Numbers for iPad

CHRIS FEHILY

 Peachpit Press

Visual QuickStart Guide
Numbers for iPad
Chris Fehily

Peachpit Press
1249 Eighth Street
Berkeley, CA 94710
510/524-2178
800/283-9444
510/524-2221 (fax)

Find us on the Web at www.peachpit.com.
To report errors, please send a note to errata@peachpit.com.
Peachpit Press is a division of Pearson Education.

Executive Editor: Clifford Colby
Editor: Dan Foster, Scribe Tribe
Production Coordinator: Myrna Vladic
Compositor: Jerry Ballew
Indexer: Jack Lewis
Cover Design: The Visual Group
Interior Design: Peachpit Press

ISBN-13: 978-0-321-75140-9
ISBN-10:   0-321-75140-X

9 8 7 6 5 4 3 2 1

Printed and bound in the United States of America

Contents at a Glance

Table of Contents

1

Getting Started

The iPad is best known for consuming stuff (music, videos, ebooks, websites, games, and so on), but Apple's iWork apps let you create stuff. The iWork trio of apps includes Pages, for word processing, Keynote, for presentations, and—the subject of this book—Numbers, for spreadsheets.

Numbers lacks the extensive features of its bigger brothers—Microsoft Excel and Numbers for Mac—and isn't meant to replace them, but it's tuned to work with the iPad's multi-touch interface, occupies little space, and is adept at the important things: data entry, tables, formulas, functions, charts, and formatting. You also can share your spreadsheets and annotate or embellish them with photos, shapes, text boxes, and movies. This book uses step-by-step instructions with plenty of screenshots to show you how to use these features, and offers workarounds and alternatives for problem areas.

iPad Basics

This book focuses on using Numbers and assumes that you know the basics of using your iPad, including:

- Your iPad's physical buttons and ports
- Typing on the onscreen keyboard
- Connecting your iPad to a computer and syncing with iTunes
- Connecting your iPad to the Internet

You can refer to this section for a refresher if you get stuck on an iPad touchscreen gesture or don't understand a technical term.

TIP iPad basics are covered in the *iPad User Guide*. To read it, tap the bookmark in Safari or go to help.apple.com/ipad.

Home Screen

After you unlock your iPad, the Home screen appears and displays icons for your apps (also called applications or programs). The iPad comes with built-in apps (Calendar, Settings, Safari, and Mail, for example) and you can download more—including Numbers—from the App Store, Apple's online store. If you add a lot of apps, new Home screens sprout automatically to display them. You should put your most frequently used apps in the Dock, which remains visible at the bottom of every Home screen. The row of small dots above the Dock indicates how many screens you have and which one you're on. Flick left or right to switch among the screens, or tap to the left or right of the dots. To go to the first Home screen, press the Home button Ⓐ.

Home button

Ⓐ App icons on the Home screen.

TABLE 1.1 MULTI-TOUCH GESTURES

To	Do This
Tap	Gently tap the screen with one fingertip.
Double-tap	Tap twice quickly (double-tap too slowly and the iPad interprets it as two single taps, which isn't the same thing).
Touch and hold	Touch the screen with your fingertip and maintain contact with the glass (typically, until some onscreen action happens).
Drag	Touch and hold a point on the screen, and then slide your fingertip across the glass to a different part of the screen.
Flick (or Swipe)	Decisively and fluidly whip your fingertip across the screen.
Pinch	Touch your thumb and index finger to the screen and pinch them together (to zoom out) or spread them apart (to zoom in).
Rotate	Spread your thumb and index finger and touch them to the screen, and then rotate them clockwise or counter-clockwise.

Two-Handed Input

The iPad's dense grid of touch-sensors spans the entire screen, so you can use two hands when the situation calls for it. In Numbers, for example, you can use both hands to type on any of the onscreen keyboards. Or you can touch and hold a shape with the finger of one hand, and then use your other hand to tap other shapes to select them all as a group.

If you're having trouble with a gesture, make sure that you're not touching the screen's edge with a stray thumb or finger (of either hand).

TIP To rearrange your icons, touch and hold any app icon for a few seconds until all the icons wiggle. Drag icons to new locations within a screen or off the edge of one screen and onto the next. Press the Home button to stop the wiggling and save your arrangement.

TIP From the first Home screen, flicking left to right will land you on the iPad's Search screen, which will find Numbers itself but, sadly, not your spreadsheet files.

TIP To change the behavior of the Home button, tap Settings > General > Home. To reset the Home screen to its original layout, tap Settings > General > Reset > Reset Home Screen Layout.

Multi-Touch Gestures

You interact with Numbers (and all iPad software) by using your fingertips to perform the touchscreen gestures described in **Table 1.1**. If you've used a computer mouse, learning these gestures will be easy because tapping, touching, and dragging correspond to similar mouse actions. Any unfamiliarity with more-advanced gestures like flicking and pinching won't last long.

TIP A drag-like gesture called a *slide* moves a control along a constrained path; you slide the iPad's unlock and volume sliders, for example.

TIP The iPad's capacitive touchscreen responds to the electric field of your fingers. Increasing finger pressure won't increase responsiveness. (And you can't wear gloves.)

TIP Apple's documentation tells you to pinch your fingers *apart*, which makes no sense but allows for pat phrases like "pinch to zoom in or out." ("Close your fingertips together to zoom out" and "Spread your fingertips apart to zoom in" would have been better descriptions.)

Getting Numbers

This section walks you through the basics of downloading, updating, and deleting Numbers.

Downloading Numbers

You can buy and download Numbers from Apple's App Store, available on the iPad itself or from iTunes on your computer. Apps that you download from the App Store and install on your iPad are backed up to your iTunes library the next time you sync. During a sync, you also can install apps on your iPad that you bought through iTunes on your computer. To use the App Store, your iPad must be connected to the Internet and you must have an iTunes Store account.

TIP **To sign in to, change, or create an iTunes Store account on your iPad, tap Settings > Store. By default, your iPad uses the iTunes account that you're signed in to when you sync with iTunes on your computer.**

Numbers Versions

This book covers Numbers for iPad version 1.1 running in iOS 3.2 on a first-generation iPad. The next version of the iPad operating system, iOS 4, adds multitasking, folders, and other odds and ends, but doesn't change how you work with Numbers.

To see your iOS version, go to the Home screen and tap Settings > General > About. The version number (and the build number, in parentheses) is listed next to the Version label. To see the version and build of Numbers, tap Settings > Numbers.

A On the iPad, the Numbers app appears in the search results under iPad Apps. To get information about Numbers—including screenshots, reviews, and version information—tap its icon instead of its price.

B In iTunes, the Numbers app appears in the search results under iPad Apps. To get information about Numbers—including screenshots, reviews, and version information—click its icon instead of its price.

To download Numbers on your iPad:

1. Tap the App Store icon on the Home screen.

2. Tap the Search field at the upper right of the screen, type *iwork* (or *numbers*), and then tap Search on the keyboard.

3. Find Numbers in the search results, tap its price, and then tap Buy App **A**.

4. Sign in to your account if requested, and then tap OK.

    A dimmed Numbers icon showing a progress meter appears on the Home screen.

5. You can flick among your Home screens or open other apps during the download.

    When the download completes, Numbers is installed immediately.

TIP To cancel a search, tap Cancel at the top left of the screen. To clear the Search field, tap the X in the Search field.

TIP If a download is interrupted, your iPad will restart the download when it reconnects to the Internet. Alternatively, you can open iTunes on your computer and complete the download to your iTunes library (provided you're signed in to the same iTunes account and your computer is connected to the Internet).

To download Numbers from iTunes on your computer:

1. On your Mac or PC, open iTunes.

2. In the iTunes sidebar, under Store, click iTunes Store.

3. Click the Search Store field at the upper right of the window, type *iwork* (or *numbers*), and then press Enter.

4. Find Numbers in the search results and then click its price **B**.

continues on next page

5. Sign in to your account if requested, and then click Buy.

While Numbers downloads, progress information appears at the top of the iTunes window and a Downloads item appears under Store in the sidebar. After the download completes, Numbers appears in your iTunes library in Apps (under Library in the sidebar) and is installed on your iPad the next time that you sync.

Updating Numbers

Developers occasionally update their apps with bug fixes, new features, and other improvements and release the changed versions through the App Store. If any updates are available, a numbered badge— denoting the number of apps to be updated— appears on the App Store icon. These updates may or may not include a Numbers update.

TIP **All updates go through the App Store; you don't have to search for them online.**

TIP **In iTunes on your computer, the updates badge appears next to Apps in the sidebar.**

TIP **To check for updates manually: In iPad, tap App Store > Updates. In iTunes, click Apps in the sidebar, and then click Check for Updates at the lower-right corner of the window.**

To update your apps:

1. Tap the App Store icon on the Home screen.

2. Tap Updates in the bottom toolbar.

A list of updated apps appears.

3. *Optional.* To learn more about an update, tap its name in the list.

Delete badge

C Deleting Numbers from the iPad.

D Deleting Numbers in iTunes.

TIP To reinstall a deleted app, re-download it from the App Store. Proceed like you're buying it again and tap the price. A dialog box will tell you that you can download it for free; tap OK.

4. To update any single app, tap Free next to its name, and then tap Install.

or

To update all your apps at once, tap Update All at the top of the screen.

When the download completes, updates are installed immediately.

Deleting Numbers

You can delete Numbers from just your iPad, from just your iTunes library, or from both. Deleting Numbers also deletes your spreadsheets; to back them up to your computer or to iWork.com, see Chapter 7.

To delete Numbers from your iPad:

1. On the Home screen, touch and hold the Numbers icon until it wiggles and an X appears in its corner **C**.

2. Tap the X, and then tap Delete.

3. Press the Home button.

To delete Numbers from iTunes on your computer:

1. On your Mac or PC, open iTunes.

2. In the iTunes sidebar, under Library, click Apps.

3. In the main section of the iTunes window, under iPad Apps, find the Numbers icon.

4. Right-click (or Control-click on Mac) the Numbers icon and choose Delete **D**.

5. Click Remove. Confirm the deletion if you're asked.

Numbers is deleted from your iPad the next time that you sync.

The Numbers Interface

To create Numbers for iPad, Apple took a scalpel to its desktop brother, Numbers for Mac, and cut away most of its menus, toolbars, palettes, and non-core features, leaving a clean workspace suitable for tap-and-drag rather than point-and-click. This section provides an overview of the Numbers interface and workspace.

To open Numbers:

Tap the Numbers icon on your iPad's Home screen.

TIP You can rotate your iPad to use Numbers in portrait or landscape view.

My Spreadsheets View

The first step in using Numbers is to create or open a spreadsheet to work on, which you do from the My Spreadsheets screen. This view is where Numbers lists all the spreadsheets that you've created or imported, and where you can open, rename, delete, or export them. Think of My Spreadsheets as a "folder" for your existing spreadsheet files as well as a starting point for new ones.

To open My Spreadsheets:

If you're opening Numbers for the first time, My Spreadsheets appears automatically.

or

My Spreadsheets If you don't see My Spreadsheets, it means a spreadsheet already is open for editing; tap My Spreadsheets in the top-left corner of the screen Ⓐ.

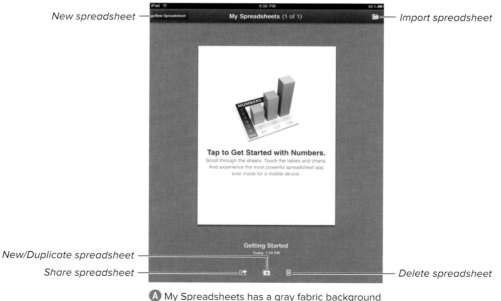

New spreadsheet — — My Spreadsheets (1 of 1) — Import spreadsheet

Tap to Get Started with Numbers.
Scroll through the sheets. Touch the tables and charts. And experience the most powerful spreadsheet app ever made for a mobile device.

Getting Started
Today, 1:59 PM

New/Duplicate spreadsheet — — Delete spreadsheet
Share spreadsheet —

Ⓐ My Spreadsheets has a gray fabric background and large images of the first page of each of your spreadsheets.

New spreadsheet. Tap New Spreadsheet to create a new spreadsheet from one of the prebuilt templates. See "Spreadsheets" in Chapter 2.

Import spreadsheet. Tap 📁 to import a spreadsheet from your computer via iTunes. See "Exporting and Importing Spreadsheets via iTunes" in Chapter 7.

Share spreadsheet. Tap 📤 to append a spreadsheet as an email attachment, export it to your computer, or upload it to iWork.com. See Chapter 7.

New/Duplicate spreadsheet. Tap ⊞ to either create a new spreadsheet or duplicate the one currently selected. See "Spreadsheets" in Chapter 2.

Delete spreadsheet. Tap 🗑 to delete the currently selected spreadsheet. See "Spreadsheets" in Chapter 2.

TIP The generic name for the My Spreadsheets screen is the *Document Manager*. Each iWork app has its own Document Manager; in Pages, it's called My Documents, and in Keynote, My Presentations.

TIP Numbers comes with a spreadsheet named Getting Started (visible in Ⓐ). You can tap it and browse its sheets to learn the essentials of Numbers, all of which are covered in this book.

Viewing and Editing Spreadsheets

After you create a new spreadsheet or open an existing one in My Spreadsheets, Numbers opens that spreadsheet in a new screen for you to view or edit. Spreadsheets share a set of controls at the top of the screen **B**.

My Spreadsheets. Tap My Spreadsheets to save your spreadsheet and return to the My Spreadsheets screen.

Undo/Redo. To undo your last change, tap Undo . To redo the last change that you undid, touch and hold Undo, and then tap Redo. You also can shake your iPad to bring up the Undo/Redo dialog box **C**.

Sheet tabs. Sheets, which divide spreadsheet information into manageable groups, are shown as a row of tabs. To add a new sheet, tap ✚ at the end of the row. See "Sheets" in Chapter 2.

My Spreadsheets   *Undo/Redo*   *Sheet tabs*   *Insert*   *Info*   *Tools*

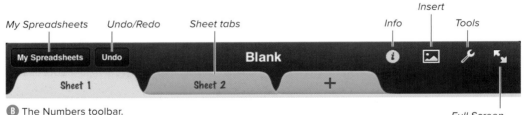

B The Numbers toolbar.

Full Screen

C Numbers stores your last few hundred actions, so you can undo and redo them when you touch and hold the Undo button (left) or shake your iPad (right). The iPad's accelerometer recognizes an intentional shaking motion — shaking front-to-back works better than shaking side-to-side.

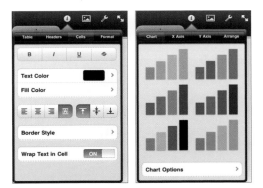

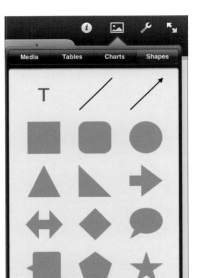

D With a table selected (left), the **ⓘ** menu displays a four-tabbed box for changing the color, style, and format of the table and its cells. With a chart selected (right), the **ⓘ** menu gives you color and style options for the chart's colors, axes, and text.

E In the 🖼 menu, tap a tab (Media, Tables, Charts, or Shapes), flick left or right within the menu to find a style you like, and then touch and hold the object and drag it to your spreadsheet.

Info. Tap **ⓘ** to change the style of tables, charts, text boxes, and other spreadsheet objects. The options change depending on what you've selected **D**.

Insert. Tap 🖼 to add photos, tables, charts, text boxes, and geometric shapes to your spreadsheet **E**.

Tools. Tap 🔧 to use Numbers' miscellaneous commands. Find searches your spreadsheet for all instances of a particular word or phrase, and optionally replaces each occurrence with new text. Go to Help launches Apple's online Numbers manual in the Safari browser. Edge Guides are thin lines that appear temporarily to help you align objects as you resize them or drag them around the screen. Check Spelling underlines typos in red **F**.

continues on next page

F The 🔧 menu holds commands that don't quite fit in the other menus.

Full Screen. Tap ![icon] to view your spread-sheet in uncluttered, full-screen glory ⓖ.

Mortgage Calculator

Replace the bold values in the Mortgage Details table with your own values. The other values are calculated for you.

Mortgage Details

Purchase price	$350,000
% down payment	10%
Down payment	$35,000
Loan amount	$315,000
Interest rate	5.50%
Mortgage length (years)	30
Payment with principal	$1,789

Monthly Payment by Interest Rate

Possible Payments

Interest Rate/Loan Amount	5.00%	5.25%	5.50%	5.75%	6.00%
$243,741	$1,308	$1,346	$1,384	$1,422	$1,461
$256,569	$1,377	$1,417	$1,457	$1,497	$1,538
$270,073	$1,450	$1,491	$1,533	$1,576	$1,619
$284,288	$1,526	$1,570	$1,614	$1,659	$1,704
$299,250	$1,606	$1,652	$1,699	$1,746	$1,794
$315,000	$1,691	$1,739	$1,789	$1,838	$1,889
$330,750	$1,776	$1,826	$1,878	$1,930	$1,983
$347,288	$1,864	$1,918	$1,972	$2,027	$2,082
$364,652	$1,958	$2,014	$2,070	$2,128	$2,186
$382,884	$2,055	$2,114	$2,174	$2,234	$2,296
$402,029	$2,158	$2,220	$2,283	$2,346	$2,410

ⓖ Tap ![icon] to hide the toolbar and focus on the data within a single sheet. Tap anywhere on the screen to exit full-screen view.

Objects

In Numbers, *objects* are the building blocks of spreadsheets—they're the design elements that you slide across the sheet canvas to create your layout. Numbers objects include tables, charts, text boxes, shapes, and photos, which you can select, move, resize, rotate, copy, delete, layer, style, and manipulate by using the same basic techniques common to all iWork programs.

If you're coming from Microsoft Excel, you may be surprised that even tables are objects. In contrast to Excel, which presents you with a huge grid of empty rows and columns, Numbers presents you with a blank canvas to which you manually add multiple tables, each with a specific number of rows and columns.

Spreadsheet Essentials

Now that you can tap your way around the Numbers workspace, it's time to learn the basics of spreadsheets—you'll need the skills covered in this chapter to build your spreadsheets, no matter how simple or complex. A Numbers spreadsheet provides a flexible, freeform canvas that you can use to organize data, create tables and charts, manage lists, insert photos and graphics, and place text anywhere on the page. Numbers supports more than 250 math and other functions for performing complex calculations with a few taps.

If you've used other spreadsheet programs, such as Numbers for Mac, Microsoft Excel, or OpenOffice.org Calc, then Numbers for iPad will be familiar. Its features let you create great-looking spreadsheets fast—features like a touch-based interface, intelligent keyboards, table and chart styles, data-entry forms, and ready-made templates for home, school, and work.

In This Chapter

Spreadsheets

To get started with Numbers, just launch it and either open an existing spreadsheet or create a new one based on one of the predesigned templates. *Templates* contain ready-made sheets, tables, charts, formulas, and other elements—they're the quickest way to start a project because much of the work has been done for you.

Each template is intended for a specific purpose (personal, personal finance, business, or education). Even if you don't use a template for its intended purpose, you still can choose it for its looks (color scheme, fonts, and formatting) and delete its contents but not its style. If you want to build your spreadsheet from scratch, use the Blank template. Exploring the different templates can show you how the assembled tables, charts, and formulas are linked to make Numbers spreadsheets tick.

To create a new spreadsheet:

In My Spreadsheets view, tap New Spreadsheet in the top-left corner of the screen, and then tap the template you want to use .

A new spreadsheet opens 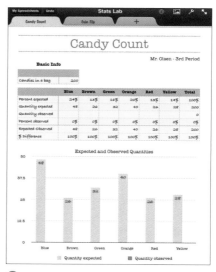.

TIP You also can create a new spreadsheet by tapping ⊞ > **New Spreadsheet** in My Spreadsheets view.

TIP Editing a spreadsheet doesn't affect the template on which it's based. You can't edit or delete the built-in templates or add custom ones.

A Flick up or down to see all the templates. The Blank template gives you only a short, empty table. The other templates contain a mix of placeholder data, charts, text, and images.

B Tap or double-tap to edit the placeholder data and objects in your new spreadsheet. Numbers has no manual Save command—changes are saved automatically about every 30 seconds. If you make a mistake, use the Undo command in the top-left corner of the screen.

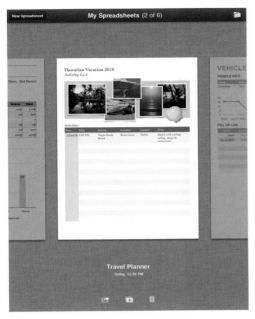

Hawaiian Vacation 2010
Activity List

VEHICLE
VEHICLE INFO

Activities

FILL UP LOG

Travel Planner
Today, 12:08 PM

C Flick with your fingers on the spreadsheet previews and not on the empty areas. Each preview shows the spreadsheet's first sheet, name, and modification time.

To open an existing spreadsheet:

In My Spreadsheets view, flick left or right to the preview of the spreadsheet that you want to open, and then tap it **C**.

The spreadsheet opens.

TIP To import a spreadsheet that you created elsewhere, see Chapter 7.

To create a copy of a spreadsheet:

1. In My Spreadsheets view, flick left or right to the preview of the spreadsheet that you want to copy.

2. Tap [+] > Duplicate Spreadsheet.

To rename a spreadsheet:

1. In My Spreadsheets view, flick left or right to the preview of the spreadsheet that you want to rename.

2. Tap its name.

   A blinking insertion point appears.

3. Type a new name. You can double-tap the name to open a pop-up menu of editing commands, or drag across the text to move the insertion point.

4. When you're done typing, tap [⌨] or Done on the keyboard to dismiss the keyboard.

To delete a spreadsheet:

1. In My Spreadsheets view, flick left or right to the preview of the spreadsheet that you want to delete.

2. Tap [🗑] > Delete Spreadsheet.

   You can't undo this action.

Tables

A *table* is a grid of rows and columns used to organize, analyze, and present data. At each row–column intersection is a *cell*, which holds an individual data value: a number, text, a date, the result of a formula, and so on. Every table has a name that optionally can be displayed above the table. You can change the default names (Table 1, Table 2, and so on) to something more descriptive.

Tables typically are where you spend most of your time when building a spreadsheet. You can add as many tables as you like to a spreadsheet, though it's not uncommon to have spreadsheets where a single table is the only object.

TIP To layer tables with other objects on the sheet, see "Arranging Objects" in Chapter 6.

To add a table to a spreadsheet:

1. Tap ![icon] in the toolbar, and then tap Tables **A**.

2. Tap the table style that's closest to what you want to use. To see all the table styles, flick right or left in the Tables window **B**.

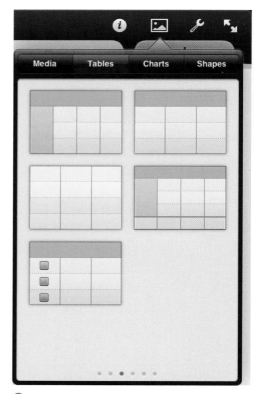

A Choose from a range of preset table styles in different arrangements and colors that match the template you're working in.

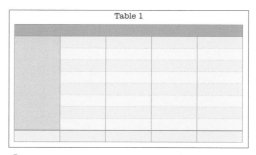

B A new, empty table appears on the sheet with a preset number of rows and columns. Whatever the look of the table you begin with, you can customize it however you wish.

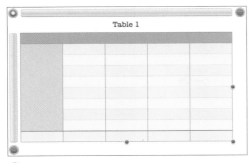

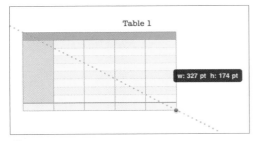

C Table handles appear when a table is selected.

D As you resize the table, edge guides appear to help you align the table with other objects. A pop-up label shows the dimensions of the resized table.

To select a table:

Tap the table **C**.

To move a table on a sheet:

1. Tap the table to select it.

2. Drag ◉ in the top-left corner of the table to position the table on the sheet.

To resize a table:

1. Tap the table to select it.

2. Tap ◉ in the top-left corner of the table and then drag one of the blue selection handles on the table's perimeter **D**.

To change the style of a table:

1. Tap the table to select it.

2. Tap **i** in the toolbar and then tap the Table tab.

3. To change the color scheme, tap a table style in the Table window **E**.

continues on next page

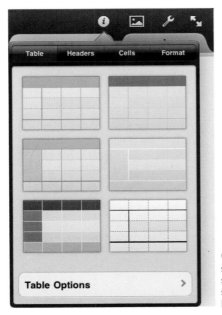

E Changing a table's color scheme won't change its structure; the table keeps the same number of rows, columns, headers, or footers.

4. To show or hide the table name, table border, alternating row colors, or grid lines, or to adjust fonts, tap Table Options at the bottom of the Table window and then set your preferences in the Table Options window **F**.

To cut, copy, or delete a table:

1. Tap the table to select it.

2. Tap ⊙ in the top-left corner of the table and then tap Cut, Copy, or Delete in the pop-up menu **G**.

To rename a table:

1. Tap the table to select it.

2. If necessary, show the table name: Tap **i** > Table > Table Options > Table Name > ON (refer to **F**) and then tap the table again to reselect it.

3. Double-tap the table name.

A blinking insertion point appears.

4. Type a new name **H**.

5. When you're done typing, tap ⌨ or Done on the keyboard to dismiss the keyboard.

G Cut removes the table so that it can be moved (pasted) elsewhere. Copy copies a table so that it can be duplicated (pasted) elsewhere, leaving the original table intact. Delete clears the table and all its data. To paste a cut or copied table, go to the destination (which can be in a different sheet or spreadsheet), tap an empty area on the sheet, and then tap Paste in the pop-up menu.

F You may need to flick up in a window to see all its options (the Table Font menu, for example, is quite long). When you're done, tap off the window or, to backtrack to other options, tap ⬅ at the top of the window.

H You can double-tap the table name to open a pop-up menu of editing commands. To format the name, select a range of text and then tap **i**.

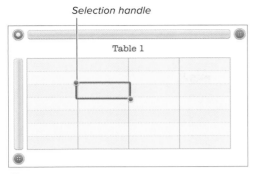
Selection handle

Table 1

A A heavy border surrounds a selected cell. The blue dots in the corners of the border are called selection handles.

Table 1

B This selection spans four rows and three columns. You can release the selection handles and then drag them again to change the selected range.

Cells

A cell is an individual box within a table that can hold a data value and is identified by the intersection of its row and column. This section shows the basics of selecting cells. (To edit the contents of cells, see Chapter 3.)

To select a cell:

Tap the cell **A**.

To select a range of cells:

1. Tap any cell in the range.

2. Drag the selection handles in any direction (up, down, left, right, or diagonally) to encompass the cells that you want to select **B**.

TIP Selection handles won't appear when the onscreen keyboard is open. Tap Done to close the keyboard.

TIP Dragging a selection handle near the edge of the screen autoscrolls the selection in the direction of the drag.

Rows and Columns

You can add, delete, select, resize, and rearrange the rows and columns of a table. A table's overall size changes as you add or delete rows or columns. If you have other tables or objects on the sheet, Numbers nudges them relative to the resized table, preventing the table from colliding with those objects when it gets larger, or from creating too much space between objects when it gets smaller.

You can label your table data by designating *header rows and columns*, which are formatted to stand out from the actual data (the *body rows and columns*). Header rows are anchored directly above the topmost body row, with their cells labeling the columns below. Header columns are directly to the left of the leftmost body column, with their cells labeling the rows to the right. When you print a table, its headers appear on each page, making long tables easier to read. You can keep the data labels in view by *freezing* header rows or columns. When you scroll through a table, frozen headers remain visible at the edge of the table, floating above the rest of the table.

You can use *footer rows* when you want to draw attention to the bottom rows of a table. Footer rows are formatted so that they stand out from the other (body) rows and typically are used to call out sums and averages under columns of numbers.

To select entire rows or columns:

1. Tap the table to select it.

    The table handles appear.

2. Tap the gray bar to the left of the row or above the column that you want to select 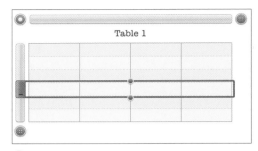.

Ⓐ When you select a row or column, you can manage masses of data easily—move or copy the selection to a new location in the table, delete the whole row or column, format or style all the cells in the selection, and more.

Selection handle

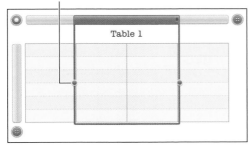

Table 1

B Drag the selection handles to expand or shrink the selection.

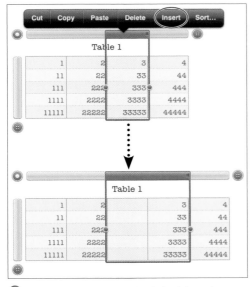

| | Cut | Copy | Paste | Delete | Insert | Sort... |

Table 1

1	2	3	4
11	22	33	44
111	222	333	444
1111	2222	3333	4444
11111	22222	33333	44444

Table 1

1	2		3	4
11	22		33	44
111	222		333	444
1111	2222		3333	4444
11111	22222		33333	44444

C A column is inserted to the left of the column that you selected.

3. To extend the selection, drag the selection handles (blue dots) to encompass the rows or columns that you want to select **B**.

To add or delete columns:

1. Tap the table to select it.

   The table handles appear.

2. Do any of the following:

   ▸ To add more columns on the right side of the table, drag ⊕ rightward.

   ▸ To delete empty columns on the right side of the table, drag ⊕ leftward. (Numbers prevents you from deleting data-containing columns accidentally with an impulsive swipe.)

   ▸ To add a column anywhere in the table, select a column, tap the gray bar above the selected column again, and then tap Insert in the pop-up menu **C**.

     If you're adding a leftmost column, tap an option to specify whether you want it to be a body or header column.

   ▸ To delete columns anywhere in the table, select a column or range of columns, tap the gray bar above the selected columns again, and then tap Delete.

To add or delete rows:

1. Tap the table to select it.

   The table handles appear.

2. Do any of the following:

   ▸ To add more rows to the bottom of the table, drag ⊕ downward.

   ▸ To delete empty rows at the bottom of the table, drag ⊕ upward. (Numbers prevents you from deleting data-containing rows accidentally with an impulsive swipe.)

   ▸ To add a row anywhere in the table, select a row, tap the gray bar on the selected row again, and then tap Insert in the pop-up menu. A row is inserted above the row that you selected.

   If you're adding a topmost or bottom-most row, tap an option to specify whether you want it to be a body, header, or footer row.

   ▸ To delete rows anywhere in the table, select a row or range of rows, tap the gray bar on the left of the selected rows again, and then tap Delete ⓓ.

To move rows or columns:

1. Tap the table to select it.

   The table handles appear.

2. Select the rows or columns that you want to move, touch and hold the blue part of the bar adjacent to the selection until the selection rises out of the table, and then drag to a new position in the table ⓔ.

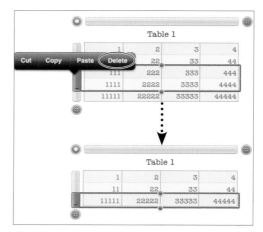

ⓓ Every column and row has its own pop-up menu, summoned with a tap on the adjacent gray bar. If you select multiple rows or columns, the Insert command doesn't appear.

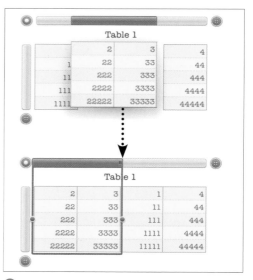

ⓔ As you drag the selection, existing rows or columns slide out of the way. (You can't use this maneuver to overwrite data, as you would with cut, copy, and paste.)

Resize handle

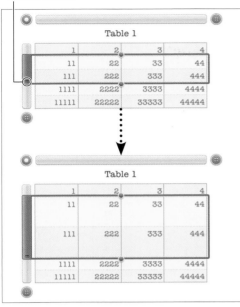

F If you select a range of rows or columns, they'll all be resized to the same height or width.

G You can add as many headers as the table will allow, as long as at least one body row and column remains.

To resize rows or columns:

1. Tap the table to select it.

   The table handles appear.

2. Select the row(s) or column(s) that you want to resize.

3. Do any of the following:

   ▸ To resize rows, drag the bottom edge of the blue bar on the left of a selected row upward or downward **F**.

   ▸ To resize columns, drag the right edge of the blue bar above a selected column leftward or rightward.

To add or delete header rows, header columns, or footer rows:

1. Tap the table to select it.

   The table handles appear.

2. Tap 🖾 in the toolbar and then tap Headers **G**.

continues on next page

3. Tap the header and footer arrows and slide the freeze controls for the items that you want to adjust Ⓗ.

TIP **When a table has both header rows and header columns, they share cells where they intersect in the top-left corner of the table. Those shared cells are considered to be part of the header row (as shown in Ⓗ).**

Table 1

ID	Col1	Col2	Col3	Col4
Row1	1	2	3	4
Row2	11	22	33	44
Row3	111	222	333	444
Row4	1111	2222	3333	4444
Row5	11111	22222	33333	44444
Total	12345	24690	37035	49380
Average	2469	4938	7407	9876

Table 1

ID	Col1	Col2	Col3	Col4
Row1	1	2	3	4
Row2	11	22	33	44
Row3	111	222	333	444
Row4	1111	2222	3333	4444
Row5	11111	22222	33333	44444
Total	12345	24690	37035	49380
Average	2469	4938	7407	9876

Ⓗ The color scheme changes automatically to highlight the headers and footers. The top table has no headers or footers. The bottom table has one header row, one header column, and two footer rows. Existing rows or columns are converted to headers or footers.

Sheets

Sheets let you divide information into manageable groups. You can, for example, place tables of raw data on one sheet and charts, summary statistics, and conclusions on another. You also can use sheets to segregate data: business contacts on one sheet and friends and family on another. Think of sheets as tabs or subdivisions within your spreadsheet, like chapters in a book—each new sheet that you add is a blank canvas ready for tables, charts, text boxes, and other objects. The quickest way to get ideas for organizing sheets is to review the templates that came with Numbers **A**.

A Sheets are shown as a row of tabs at the top of the screen (these sheets are from the built-in templates). Every new sheet is given a default name (Sheet 1, Sheet 2, and so on) that you can change to something more descriptive.

B If you have no tables in your spreadsheet, tapping **+** will create a new sheet immediately, without showing you this menu.

C The bright-colored tab indicates the active (frontmost) sheet.

> **TIP** A sheet scrolls downward and to the right, beyond the last objects on it.

> **TIP** Despite its name, you shouldn't think of a sheet as a single page; large sheets can span several pages when printed.

To add a new sheet:

Tap the **+** tab at the top of the screen, at the end of the row of tabs, and then tap New Sheet **B**.

You can add as many sheets as you want within a spreadsheet.

To move from sheet to sheet:

Flick or drag to scroll the tabs along the top of the screen and then tap a tab to open its sheet **C**.

To rename a sheet:

Double-tap the sheet's tab at the top of the screen and then type a new name.

> **TIP** Sheets within the same spreadsheet all must have different names. Numbers will cancel your edit if you type a duplicate name.

To reorder sheets:

Touch and hold the sheet's tab until its color darkens slightly, and then drag it left or right to a new position in the row of tabs .

TIP If you're moving a sheet a short distance, you can hold-and-flick (rather than hold-and-drag) its tab.

TIP You can't move a sheet while you're renaming it (that is, while the insertion point is blinking within the tab's text). Tap outside the text.

To delete a sheet:

1. Tap the sheet's tab to open the sheet.

2. Tap the tab again, and then tap Delete in the pop-up menu **E**.

To make a copy of a sheet:

1. Tap the sheet's tab to open the sheet.

2. Tap the tab again, and then tap Duplicate in the pop-up menu **F**.

D The other tabs slide to make way for the one you're dragging. If you want to move a sheet to a position that's not currently visible, drag its tab off the left or right edge of the screen to autoscroll the tabs.

E If the sheet that you delete contains a table whose data are displayed as a chart in another sheet, then the links are severed and the chart reverts to a placeholder chart.

F The copy appears alongside the original, with a slightly different name.

3

Data Entry

The first task in building a spreadsheet is to enter your raw data into table cells. Each cell holds an individual value: a number, text, a date, or a duration. (Formulas, which are mathematical and functional expressions that resolve to values, are covered in the next chapter.) Numbers provides specialized onscreen keyboards that pop up when you edit a cell's contents. You also can do the usual operations common to many spreadsheets: copy and move cells, fill series of values, edit lists via data-entry forms, and sort rows. This chapter describes how to work with cells and their contents. (To import your data rather than typing it directly into Numbers, see Chapter 7).

In This Chapter

Editing and Formatting Cells

A virtual keyboard appears on the screen whenever you tap inside a cell (or any editable area) **A**. After you type a value in a cell, you can apply a format to that cell to display its value in a particular way. Applying a currency format, for example, displays a currency symbol (such as $, £, or ¥) in front of numbers in cells. To make a cell stand out, you can change its style (typeface, color, alignment, border, and so on).

A One of Numbers' virtual keyboards appears at the bottom of the screen when needed. The text keyboard is shown here.

Virtual Keyboarding

Typing on the virtual keyboard is straightforward (and familiar to iPhone or iPod touch users). Numbers' keyboards have the same features as the standard iPad keyboards:

- Keyboards reorient for portrait and landscape views.

- You can touch and hold certain keys to see variants of their characters in a pop-up display. The E key, for example, displays not only the standard e but also é, è, ê, and ë.

- In the text keyboard, tap the .?123 key to see the numbers and most punctuation; within that layout, tap the #+= key to see less-common characters, tap 123 to return to the numbers-and-punctuation layout, or tap ABC to return to the alphabetic keys.

- A quick way to type a character on an alternative text keyboard is to touch and hold the .?123 or #+= key and (still touching the screen) slide your finger up to the character that you want, and then lift your finger. (Characters are input only when you lift your finger.)

- To delete the last character that you typed, tap ⌫.

- To dismiss the keyboard, tap ⌨ or Done, or tap outside of the onscreen keyboard.

- To adjust keyboard behavior, on your Home screen, tap Settings > General > Keyboard.

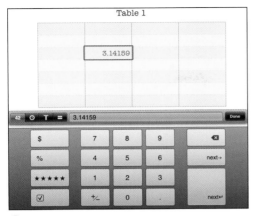

Table 1

B You enter different types of data by using Numbers' different keyboards, accessed by tapping the buttons on the left side of the formula bar (just above the keyboard). The numeric keyboard **42** is shown here. You can use the other keyboards to enter dates, times, and durations **⌖**; text **T**; or formulas **☰**.

To edit the contents of a cell:

Double-tap the cell and use the keyboard to type your data **B**.

TIP You can move from cell to cell when editing cell contents. To move to the cell to the right of the current cell, tap **→** on the keyboard (if you're in the last cell of a row, a column is added). To move to the first cell below the current cell or row, tap **↵** (if you're in the last cell of a column, a row is added). To enter text, just tap the desired cell and start typing (**→** and **↵** won't display on the **T** keyboard).

TIP If you're editing a formula, you can tap **•••** to show the buttons for the other keyboards.

Selecting and Editing Text

You can select any portion of text within a cell to edit it.

- When you tap text in the formula bar, a blinking insertion point indicates where new text will appear when you type.

- To move the insertion point, touch and hold near where you want to place it until a magnifying glass appears, and then drag over the text to the new position and lift your finger.

- To select a word, double-tap it. To select a paragraph, triple-tap it.

- To extend or shorten the range of selected text, select a word and then drag the blue drag points to encompass the characters that you want to select.

- To cut or copy text, select a range of text, tap Cut or Copy, and then move the insertion point (or select some text to replace) and tap Paste.

To delete the contents of cells:

Select a cell or a range of cells, tap the selection, and then tap Delete 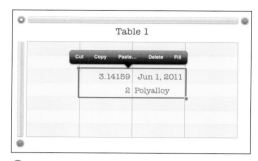.

To format cells:

1. Select a cell or a range of cells to format.

2. Tap ⓘ in the toolbar and then tap the Format tab **D**.

3. To apply a default format quickly, tap a format name in the Format list.

   or

   To set options for a format, tap ⓔ at the right of the name in the Format list and set the options described in Table 3.1

   Cell values update instantly to reflect the formatting options that you choose **F**.

C A pop-up menu of editing commands appears when you tap a selection.

D If the selected cell has formatting already applied, a checkmark in the Format list identifies the cell's format. If you've selected a range of formatted cells, the format of only the first cell is indicated.

TABLE 3.1 Cell Format Options

Format	Options
Number	In the Number Options window **E**, tap Number for standard number formatting. Tap the arrows to set the number of decimal places. Slide Separator to show or hide thousands separators. Tap an option to set the appearance of negative values. Tap Scientific to make numbers appear in scientific notation. Tap Fraction to make numbers appear with a numerator and denominator.
Currency	In the Currency Options window, tap the arrows to set the number of decimal places. Slide Separator to show or hide thousands separators. Slide Accounting Style to position the currency symbol. Tap Currency to select a currency symbol. Tap an option to set the appearance of negative values.
Percentage	In the Percentage Options window, tap the arrows to set the number of decimal places. Slide Separator to show or hide the thousands separators. Tap an option to set the appearance of negative values.
Date & Time	In the Date & Time Options window, tap the Date format and the Time format that you want. Flick up in the window to see all the options.
Duration	In the Duration Options window, drag the left or right end of the duration range selector to encompass the scale of the time duration that you want to use, from weeks (Wk) to milliseconds (Ms). Under Format, select None to display no time units, Short to display time units as abbreviations, or Long to spell out the entire time units.

Number Options

Number | Scientific | Fraction

Decimals **2**

Separator ON

100
-100 ✓
(100)
(100)

E When you're done, tap off the window or, to backtrack to other options, tap ⬅ at the top of the window.

TIP Use the Text format for alphanumeric text. Use the Checkbox format when a value can have one of two states (see the "Checkboxes" sidebar). Use the Star Rating format to display the integers 0–5 as a number of star symbols; to change a star rating, tap a star or dot (or double-tap the cell and then tap ★ ★ ★ • • in the formula bar). Star ratings, like checkboxes, can be used in mathematical formulas and sorting operations.

TIP You can format empty cells. When you enter a value in the cell, it is displayed using the cell's format. Clearing a cell (backspacing over its contents) removes its value but not its formatting; deleting the contents (tapping Delete in the pop-up menu) removes both.

TIP The buttons in the left column of the numeric keyboard offer a quick way to change formats (refer to **B**).

TIP A formatted cell automatically displays the correct keyboard for its data type.

Table 1		
1.2	Oct 1, 2011	1w 2d 3h
1.200	10/1/2011 12:00 AM	1 week 2 days 3 hours
1.20E+00	Sat, Oct 1, 2011	1:2:3
1 1/5	10/1/2011	1w 2d
$1.20	1-Oct-2011	9 days 3 hours
€ 1.2000	1-Oct	219h
120.0%	Oct-11	9 days

F Formatting determines only how cell values are displayed; it doesn't change the data. The three columns in this table show the same value of a number, a date, and a duration, respectively, formatted differently. When a cell is used in a formula, its actual value is used, not its formatted value.

Checkboxes

A checkbox indicates one of two states: yes or no, on or off, complete or incomplete, for or against, alive or dead, and so on. These *Boolean values*, as programmers call them, are a simple choice of TRUE or FALSE. In Numbers, you use checkboxes to toggle a cell's value between TRUE (✔️, checked) and FALSE (⬜ , unchecked). To toggle the value of a checkbox, double-tap the cell to edit it, and then either tap the cell again or tap (true) or (false) in the formula bar. The built-in Checklist template shows a common use for checkboxes: a to-do list.

In mathematical formulas and sorting operations, the checkbox value of TRUE is 1 (one) and FALSE is 0 (zero). If you sum a column of checkboxes, for example, the result is the number of checkboxes that are checked. It's also common to multiply by a checkbox to force the result to be zero if the box is unchecked.

To style cells:

1. Select a cell or a range of cells to style.

2. Tap ⓘ in the toolbar, and then tap the Cells tab ⓖ.

3. Do any of the following:

   ▸ Tap a typeface button to apply bold, italic, underline, or strikethrough.

   ▸ Tap the color buttons to choose the text and background colors (flick left in a color window to see all the colors).

   ▸ Tap the alignment buttons on the left to align text horizontally within the cell: left, center, right, or justified. The alignment buttons on the right align text vertically within the cell: top, middle, or bottom.

   ▸ Tap Border Style to put a border around the cells.

   ▸ Slide Wrap Text in Cell to set whether a value in a cell can spill into adjacent, empty cells.

Cell values update instantly to reflect the style options that you choose ⓗ.

ⓖ Like cell formats, cell styles determine only how cell values are displayed; the data aren't affected.

ⓗ Avoid using too many formats and styles.

Copying and Moving Cells

You can copy or move cells within a table, to another table, or to an empty area on a sheet to create a new table. (For details about selecting cells, see "Cells" in Chapter 2.)

To copy cells:

1. Select the range of cells that you want to copy.

2. Tap the selection, and then tap Copy **Ⓐ**.

continues on next page

Cut	Copy	Paste	Delete	Fill			
1	2	3					
4	5	6					
7	8	9					
10	11	12					

Ⓐ A pop-up menu of editing commands appears when you tap selected cells.

Cut, Copy, and Paste Basics

Cut-and-paste removes (cuts) information and places it on the clipboard so that it can be moved (pasted) elsewhere. Cutting deletes the data and formatting from its original location.

Copy-and-paste copies information to the clipboard so that it can be duplicated (pasted) elsewhere. Copying leaves the original data and formatting intact (nothing visible happens).

The *clipboard* is the invisible area of memory where Numbers stores cut or copied data, where it remains until it's overwritten when you cut or copy something else. This scheme lets you paste the same thing multiple times in different places. You can transfer information from Numbers to another program—such as Pages or Keynote—provided that program can read data generated by Numbers. Note that you can't paste something that you've deleted (as opposed to cut), because Numbers doesn't place that something on the clipboard.

3. Select the destination cell(s), tap the selection, and then tap Paste. The destination determines how Numbers pastes the clipboard contents **B**, **C**, **D**, and **E**. Numbers replaces the values and formatting of the destination cells.

or

Tap an empty area of a sheet, tap again, and then tap Paste. Numbers adds the cells to the canvas as a new table.

To move cells by pasting:

1. Select the range of cells that you want to move.

2. Tap the selection, and then tap Cut (refer to **A**).

B When you select only one destination cell, Numbers pastes the entire clipboard, using that cell as the top-left corner of the pasted cells.

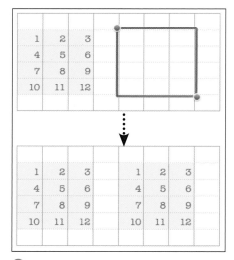

C When the selected destination has the same dimensions (that is, the same number of rows and columns) as the clipboard's contents, Numbers pastes the entire clipboard unchanged (the same as **B**).

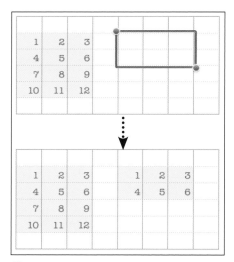

D When the selected destination has smaller dimensions than the clipboard's contents, Numbers pastes only a subset of the clipboard, starting with the top-left corner.

E When the selected destination has larger dimensions than the clipboard's contents, Numbers pastes the entire clipboard, repeating rows and columns to fill the entire destination.

F A transparent image of the original cells follows your drag. Numbers highlights the cells where the selection will land when you lift your finger.

3. Select the destination cell(s), tap the selection, and then tap Paste. The destination determines how Numbers pastes the clipboard contents. Numbers replaces the values and formatting of the destination cells.

or

Tap an empty area of a sheet, tap again, and then tap Paste. Numbers adds the cells to the canvas as a new table.

To move cells by dragging:

1. Select the range of cells that you want to move.

2. Touch and hold the selection until it rises out of the table.

3. Drag it to another location in the table **F**. (You can't drag to another table or to an empty area of the sheet.)

TIP Pasting a single cell to a range of cells will clone the original cell in every cell of the destination.

TIP You can paste cells to a table or an empty area on the same sheet, a different sheet, or a sheet in a different spreadsheet file—the contents of the clipboard don't change when you close one spreadsheet and open another.

TIP If your data range contains formulas, you're given the option of pasting the formulas or only their computed values.

Filling Cells with Data Series

The *fill* feature lets you create a column or row of values based on just one or two cells that Numbers can extrapolate into a series. Fill looks at the values that you've already entered in a row or column and infers the additional values to add. Here are examples of standard series that fill recognizes:

- Numbers that regularly increase (1, 2, 3) or decrease (−5, −10, −15)

- Letters (A, B, C)

- Days (Sunday, Monday, Tuesday) and months (Jan, Feb, Mar), either written out or in three-letter abbreviations

- Alphanumeric serial numbers, where text is followed by digits (ABC-01, ABC-02, ABC-03)

You also can use fill to copy a single cell multiple times (like a fast copy-and-paste). If you select one cell that contains a number or text that's not part of a standard series, fill will copy that value to all the target cells in the row or column.

If you start with three or more cells with an irregular interval, fill simply repeats the pattern; selecting three cells containing 6, 3, and 17, for example, fills the target cells with 6, 3, 17, 6, 3, 17, ...

xxx	xxx	xxx	xxx	xxx
888	xx	xxx	xxx	xxx
xxx	xxx	xxx	xxx	xxx

↓

xxx	xxx	xxx	xxx	xxx
888	888	888	888	xxx
xxx	xxx	xxx	xxx	xxx

A You can fill up or down along the same column or left or right along the same row, but you can't drag diagonally to fill a block of cells.

To fill a range of cells:

1. Enter the starting value(s) of the series in a row or column.

2. Select the cell(s) you just entered.

3. Tap the selection, and then tap Fill.

   A yellow box appears around the cell(s).

4. Drag a side of the yellow box along the row or column that you want to fill **A**.

   Numbers fills the row or column with the next values in the series. If any target cells already contain data, Numbers overwrites them with the new values and formats. **B** shows examples of additional fills.

TIP Fill doesn't establish an ongoing relationship among cells in the range. After filling, you can change the cells independently of each other.

TIP When you fill a formula into new cells, Numbers updates the formula's cell references to reflect the new locations. For details, see "Copying and Moving Formulas" in Chapter 4.

1	10	-4	0.0	1.33	1	Jun	Monday	S	Warp 0	1-5
	11	-2	1.5	1.66	1		Wednesday			1-10
					2					
					3					

↓

1	10	-4	0.0	1.33	1	Jun	Monday	S	Warp 0	1-5
1	11	-2	1.5	1.66	1	Jul	Wednesday	T	Warp 1	1-10
1	12	0	3.0	1.99	2	Aug	Friday	U	Warp 2	1-15
1	13	2	4.5	2.32	3	Sep	Sunday	V	Warp 3	1-20
1	14	4	6.0	2.65	1	Oct	Tuesday	W	Warp 4	1-25
1	15	6	7.5	2.98	1	Nov	Thursday	X	Warp 5	1-30
1	16	8	9.0	3.31	2	Dec	Saturday	Y	Warp 6	1-35
1	17	10	10.5	3.64	3	Jan	Monday	Z	Warp 7	1-40
1	18	12	12.0	3.97	1	Feb	Wednesday	A	Warp 8	1-45
1	19	14	13.5	4.30	1	Mar	Friday	B	Warp 9	1-50

B These before-and-after shots show the results of filling columns with different starting values. Note the series in column 5—filling decimal (floating-point) numbers can lead to unexpected results due to rounding.

Using Forms to Edit Lists

A *form* is a view of a table (a special sheet) designed for quick and easy data entry. When you link a table to a form, Numbers automatically updates each row in the table as you enter information on the form— each table row is shown as a single page on the form. If you make any changes to the table directly, such as editing cells, adding or deleting columns, or changing data types, the form self-updates to match those changes. Forms work best with large tables, when it would be cumbersome to navigate rows, read across columns, and edit data directly in the table.

To create and use a form:

1. Make sure that the table for which you want to create a form has a header row. A header column is optional .

   For details, see "Rows and Columns" in Chapter 2.

2. Tap the **+** tab at the top of the screen, at the end of the row of sheet tabs, and then tap New Form.

3. If your spreadsheet has several tables, a list of tables appears. Tap the name of the target table.

4. In the form that appears , do any of the following:

   ▸ To edit a value, tap it.

   ▸ To go to the next row in the table, tap ⊙. To go to the previous row, tap ⊖.

   ▸ To navigate rows quickly, drag up or down the gray dots along the right side of the screen.

   ▸ To add a new row after the current row, tap **+**.

   ▸ To delete the current row, tap 🗑.

Table 1

ID	Price	Date	Check	Rating
A154	$55.00	22-Jun-2011	☐	★★ • • •
D331	$12.00	5-May-2010	☑	★★★★ •
A110	$9.99	1-Jan-2010	☑	★★★ • •
R130	$12.00	1-Jan-2011	☑	★★★★★
R129	$1,110.50	16-Mar-2009	☑	★★★★★
B999	$9.99	22-Jun-2011	☑	★★★ • •
B888	$12.00	6-Aug-2010	☑	★★ • • •
A000	$12.95	7-Dec-2010	☐	• • • • •
A999	$0.99	24-Jul-2010	☑	★★★★ •

A This table has a header row and a header column. Numbers uses headers to label values and rows in the form.

B The name of the linked table appears on the form's sheet tab. The indicator in the form's top-right corner shows the current row number and total number of rows. If the table has a header column, its (editable) values appear above the data-entry grid rather than in it.

TIP You can flick up and down a form to see all its fields.

Sorting Rows in a Table

You can order the rows in a table, making information easier to find and patterns easier to spot. A few facts about sorting:

- You can sort in ascending order (A, B, C...1, 2, 3...Jan, Feb, Mar) or descending order (Z, Y, X...3, 2, 1...Dec, Nov, Oct).

- You can sort on any data type: numbers, text, dates, checkboxes, and so on.

- Rows are ordered according to the values in a specified column.

- Entire rows stay intact when they jump to their new sorted positions in the table. Sorting on a column doesn't mean that you're sorting *only* that column—rows always keep all their column values.

- Header and footer rows don't move when a table is sorted; they stay fixed at the top and bottom of the table. (For details, see "Rows and Columns" in Chapter 2.)

To sort rows:

1. Tap the table that you want sort.

   The table handles appear.

2. Tap the gray bar above the column that you want to sort on, tap it again, and then tap Sort in the pop-up menu (A).

3. Choose whether to sort in ascending or descending order.

   Numbers sorts the rows of the table (B).

TIP Unlike Microsoft Excel and Numbers for Mac, Numbers for iPad doesn't support multi-column sorts, which are used to break ties when two or more rows have the same value in a sort column. But there's a tedious workaround: To do a multi-column sort on the columns A, B, and C, for example, work *backward*: First sort on column C, then B, and then A. This technique works because Numbers retains the order of rows when sorting tied values.

TIP Numbers does not support filtering (hiding certain categories of rows).

	Cut	Copy	Paste	Delete	Insert	Sort...

ID	Price	Date	Check	Rating
A154	$55.00	22-Jun-2011	☐	★ ★ · · ·
D331	$12.00	5-May-2010	☑	★ ★ ★ · ·
A110	$9.99	1-Jan-2010	☑	★ ★ ★ · ·
R130	$12.00	1-Jan-2011	☑	★ ★ ★ ★ ★
R129	$1,110.50	16-Mar-2009	☑	★ ★ ★ ★ ★
B999	$9.99	22-Jun-2011	☐	★ ★ ★ · ·
B888	$12.00	6-Aug-2010	☑	★ ★ · · ·
A000	$12.95	7-Dec-2010	☐	· · · · ·
A999	$0.99	24-Jul-2010	☑	★ ★ ★ ★ ·

(A) An unsorted table.

ID	Price	Date	Check	Rating
R129	$1,110.50	16-Mar-2009	☑	★ ★ ★ ★ ★
A110	$9.99	1-Jan-2010	☑	★ ★ ★ · ·
D331	$12.00	5-May-2010	☑	★ ★ ★ · ·
A999	$0.99	24-Jul-2010	☑	★ ★ ★ ★ ·
B888	$12.00	6-Aug-2010	☑	★ ★ · · ·
A000	$12.95	7-Dec-2010	☐	· · · · ·
R130	$12.00	1-Jan-2011	☑	★ ★ ★ ★ ★
A154	$55.00	22-Jun-2011	☐	★ ★ · · ·
B999	$9.99	22-Jun-2011	☐	★ ★ ★ · ·

(B) The same table sorted by the Date column in ascending order.

A The Tools menu is home to the text-editing tools.

B All instances of found text are highlighted on the sheet; the current instance is selected and highlighted in yellow.

Using Text-Editing Tools

You can find every instance of a word or phrase in your spreadsheet and optionally change it to something else. You also can find and correct misspellings and look up words in the built-in dictionary.

To find or replace text:

1. Tap 🔧 in the toolbar, and then tap Find **A**.

2. In the search field, type the text that you want to find **B**.

3. If you want to constrain the search results, tap ⚙ and slide Match Case or Whole Words.

4. If you want to replace the found text with new text, tap ⚙, tap Find and Replace, and then type the new text in the Replace field.

5. Do any of the following:

   ▸ To find the next or previous instance of the text, tap ↵ or ◀.

   ▸ To replace the current instance of the text, tap Replace.

   ▸ To replace all instances of the text, touch and hold Replace, and then tap Replace All.

   TIP You can tap in the Find and Replace fields to show a pop-up menu of the standard editing commands (cut, copy, paste, and so on).

To find and correct misspellings:

1. Tap 🔧 in the toolbar, and then slide Check Spelling to ON.

    Numbers underlines misspelled words in red.

2. To correct a misspelled word, tap it and then tap one of the suggested spellings in the pop-up menu **C**.

To look up a word in the dictionary:

Double-tap the word, tap More in the pop-up menu, and then tap Definition **D**.

The definition appears in the pop-up Dictionary window.

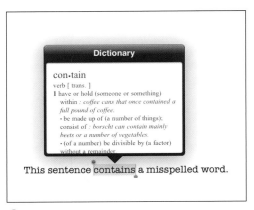

C If spelling suggestions don't appear automatically, tap More in the pop-up menu, and then tap Replace.

D Flick up in the Dictionary window to see the entire entry. You don't have to be connected to the Internet to use the dictionary.

Formulas and Functions

After you enter and organize your data values in tables, you can use formulas and functions to reduce reams of raw numbers to meaningful information. A *formula* performs a calculation and displays the result in the cell where you enter the formula, called a *formula cell*. Formulas can do things as simple as adding two numbers, but it's by using functions in formulas that you bring to bear Numbers' true computing abilities. *Functions* are built-in, named operations, such as SUM and AVERAGE, that perform a wide range of calculations for statistics, probability, dates and times, finance, engineering, text, and more.

In This Chapter

Formula Basics

A formula cell displays the result of its calculation and, on the surface, looks like any other (nonformula) cell. By just looking at a table, you can't tell the difference between a cell that contains a formula whose result is 6 and a cell that contains the number 6 (the number typed in directly). It's crucial to distinguish a formula's two display components: the formula itself and the resulting value. The actual contents of a formula cell is an equation—the formula—that tells Numbers how to generate that cell's value. It's that value, and not the formula, that's used in any calculations that refer to the cell.

To view a formula:

Double-tap the cell containing the formula.

Numbers opens the formula keyboard and displays the cell's formula in the *formula bar* above the keyboard .

Ignoring the technical details for now, take note of the basic traits common to all formulas:

- You enter each formula into a single cell. A formula can *reference* other cells on the spreadsheet, but the entire formula itself resides only in the cell where its result is displayed.

- Numbers recalculates the result of a formula every time you open a spreadsheet or change a data value that the formula uses. In , for example, if you change any Test 1 score, Numbers auto-updates the value of the formula cell showing that column's average. For small tables or simple formulas, updates occur instantly; for large tables or complex formulas, updates are slower.

- Formulas can operate on and display results in any data type: numbers, text, dates, times, durations, and Boolean (true/false) values.

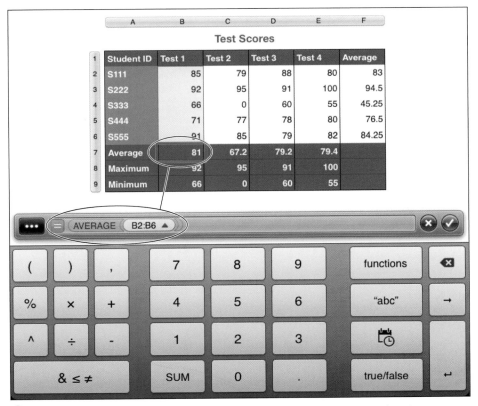

The formula bar lets you view, as well as edit, formulas. This table shows students' test scores. The selected cell in the second column (B7) shows the average score of all five students on the first test. The formula bar shows the actual contents of the cell (which uses the AVERAGE function), and the cell itself displays the formula's result (81).

Summarizing Data Quickly

Numbers lets you select a block of cells and display pop-up summary statistics and a chart—no formulas needed.

To summarize data quickly:

1. Tap ![icon] to show the spreadsheet in full-screen view.

2. Touch and hold any cell on a corner edge of the range that you want to summarize.

   A yellow box appears around the cell.

3. Drag in any direction to encompass the target cells.

   As you drag, a summary window appears showing statistics for the selected cells 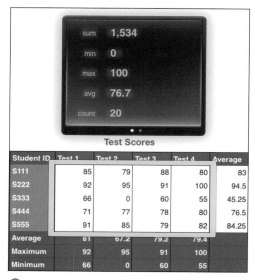.

4. Do any of the following:

   ▸ To see a line chart of the selected cells, flick left-to-right in the summary window .

   ▸ To see summaries of other ranges, touch, hold, and drag across their cells.

   ▸ To return to normal view, double-tap anywhere on the sheet.

> **TIP** You shouldn't summarize a selection of mixed data types (numbers, text, dates, and so on). If your selection contains numbers and text, for example, the count reflects all the cells, but the other statistics ignore the text cells (hence, the sum divided by the count won't equal the average).

> **TIP** Summaries also work for selections of dates, times, or durations, although the sum and average make sense only for durations. Only counts are given for a selection of Boolean values.

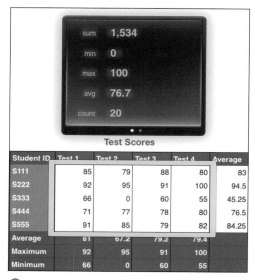

	sum	1,534
	min	0
	max	100
	avg	76.7
	count	20

Test Scores

Student ID	Test 1	Test 2	Test 3	Test 4	Average
S111	85	79	88	80	83
S222	92	95	91	100	94.5
S333	66	0	60	55	45.25
S444	71	77	78	80	76.5
S555	91	85	79	82	84.25
Average	81	67.2	79.2	79.4	
Maximum	92	95	91	100	
Minimum	66	0	60	55	

A The summary window shows the sum, minimum value, maximum value, average, and count (the number of nonempty cells) of the selected values.

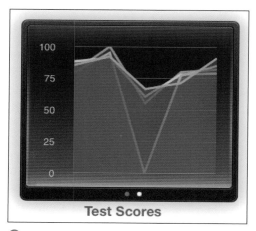

Test Scores

B The chart shows a line for each data series in the selected range. Unfortunately, you can't control whether the chart shows rows or columns as series.

Elements of Formulas

Every formula uses some combination of the following elements **A**:

Equal sign (=). The formula keyboard auto-enters the equal sign required at the start of every formula, so there's no danger of forgetting or deleting it.

Constants. Constants, also called *literals* or *static values*, are numbers, text, dates, times, durations, or Boolean (true/false) values. Constants are so called because they never change (unless you edit the formula).

continues on next page

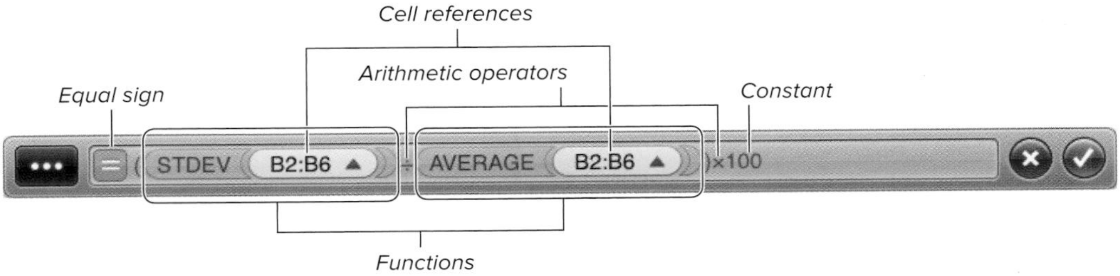

A The parts of a formula.

Arithmetic operators. These operators do basic math. The *unary operators* work on only one numeric value (**Table 4.1**); the *binary operators* work on two values (**Table 4.2**).

Cell references. These references point to the cell or range of cells whose values you need to do a calculation. For details, see "Understanding Cell References" and "Using Cell References" later in this chapter.

Comparison operators. These operators compare two values and return a Boolean (true/false) value depending on their relationship (equal, not equal, and so on). For details, see "Understanding Comparison Operators" and "Using Comparison Operators" later in this chapter.

Functions. Functions built into Numbers let you do a wide range of calculations. The TODAY function, for example, returns today's date, and STDEV calculates the sample standard deviation of a range of numbers. For details, see "Understanding Functions" and "Using Functions" later in this chapter.

TABLE 4.1 Time Unary Arithmetic Operators

Operator	Description	Example	Result
-	Reverses the sign (positive or negative) of a value	5 + -3	2
+	Leaves a value unchanged (useful only rarely)	5 - +3	2
%	Divides a value by 100	5%	0.05 (formatted as 5%)

TABLE 4.2 Binary Arithmetic Operators

Operator	Description	Example	Result
+	Adds two values	2 + 4	6
-	Subtracts the second value from the first	2 - 4	-2
x	Multiplies two values	2 x 4	8
÷	Divides the first value by the second	2 ÷ 4	0.5
^	Raises the first value to the power of the second	2 ^ 4	16

Saving a Formula

Instead of tapping ✅ to save your formula and dismiss the keyboard, you can move from cell to cell and enter more formulas. To move to the cell to the right of the current cell, tap ➡ on the keyboard (if you're in the last cell of a row, a column is added). To move to the first cell below the current cell or row, tap ↵ (if you're in the last cell of a column, a row is added).

When you finish editing a formula, *don't* tap another cell to save the formula. Recall from "Editing and Formatting Cells" in Chapter 3 that, normally, when you edit a cell's contents, tapping any other cell will save your changes and select the tapped cell. When you're editing a formula in the formula bar, however, tapping another cell inserts a reference to that cell in the formula itself.

Entering Formulas

A simple formula is =1+2. (An even simpler one is =3, but that's no different than just typing 3 in a cell.) The leading equal sign, supplied for you when you use the formula keyboard, distinguishes a formula from text, numbers, dates, and other raw values.

TIP When entering a formula, you can use most of the standard editing techniques described in "Editing and Formatting Cells" in Chapter 3.

To enter a formula in a cell:

1. Double-tap the cell.

2. If you're entering a new formula, tap ▣ on the left side of the formula bar (just above the keyboard) to open the formula keyboard.

   or

   If you're editing an existing formula, the formula keyboard opens automatically.

continues on next page

3. Position the insertion point in the formula bar or select an element to change or replace, and then do any of the following 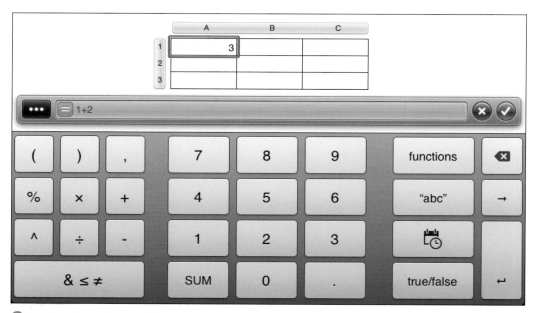:

- To insert a constant, type it. For numbers, tap the numeric keys on the formula keyboard. For text, tap the "abc" key. For dates, times, and durations, tap the 📅 key. For Boolean values, tap the true/false key (tap it repeatedly to toggle the value).

- To insert an arithmetic operator, tap its key on the left side of the formula keyboard. If the arithmetic operators aren't visible, tap the ()+÷ key.

- To insert a cell reference, see "Using Cell References" later in this chapter.

- To insert a comparison operator, see "Using Comparison Operators" later in this chapter.

- To insert a function, see "Using Functions" later in this chapter.

- To remove an element, select it or position the insertion point to the right of the element, and then tap ⌫. To remove multiple elements, you can tap repeatedly or touch and hold ⌫.

4. When you're done, tap ✓ to enter the formula, or tap ✗ to cancel and revert to the cell's previous contents.

TIP You *must* type formulas on the formula keyboard. If you use the text 🅃 keyboard and type =1+2, Numbers treats the entry as text and displays =1+2 instead of calculating the result.

TIP Tapping ⋯ on the formula bar shows buttons that open Numbers' other (nonformula) keyboards.

Ⓐ The formula bar always displays the complete formula (=1+2). The ✗ and checkmark buttons on the right side of the formula bar let you cancel or complete the formula.

TABLE 4.3 Order of Evaluation (Highest to Lowest)

Operator	Description
( )	Calculations inside parentheses
-, +, %	Unary negation, unary identity, unary percent
^	Exponentiation
×, ÷	Multiplication, division
+, -	Addition, subtraction

Determining the Order of Operations

Numbers uses rules of precedence and associativity to determine the order in which it evaluates each part of an arithmetic formula. *Precedence* determines the priority of various operators when more than one operator is used in a formula. Operations with higher precedence are performed first. The formula

=2 + 3 × 4

is 14 rather than 20 because multiplication has higher precedence than addition. Numbers first calculates 3 × 4 and then adds 2.

Operators with lower precedence are less *binding* than those with higher precedence. **Table 4.3** lists operator precedences from most to least binding. Operators in the same row of Table 4.3 have equal precedence.

Associativity determines the order of evaluation in a formula when adjacent operators have equal precedence. Numbers uses left-to-right associativity for all operators, so

=6 ÷ 2 × 3

is 9 (not 1) because 6 ÷ 2 is evaluated first, and

=2 ^ 3 ^ 2

is 64 (not 512) because 2 ^ 3 is evaluated first.

continues on next page

You can use parentheses to override precedence and associativity rules. Expressions inside parentheses are evaluated before expressions outside them. Adding parentheses to the preceding examples, you get (2 + 3) × 4 is 20, 6 ÷ (2 × 3) is 1, and 2 ^ (3 ^ 2) is 512. It's good practice to add parentheses (even when they're unnecessary) to lengthy formulas to ensure your intended evaluation order and make formulas easier to read.

=5 ^ 2 × 4 ÷ 2

is equivalent to

=((5 ^ 2) × 4) ÷ 2

but the latter is clearer.

> **TIP** Arithmetic operators have higher precedence than comparison operators but lower precedence than functions. See "Understanding Comparison Operators" and "Understanding Functions" later in this chapter.

> **TIP** Use parentheses in pairs (one closing parenthesis for every opening one). If you mismatch parentheses, Numbers flags a syntax error in your formula.

Reference-tab letters refer to columns. Reference-tab numbers refer to rows. Here, cell B2 is selected.

Understanding Cell References

Formulas involving only constants are fine when you want to use Numbers as a jumped-up pocket calculator, but the real power of formulas comes from doing calculations with the raw data that are already in your spreadsheet. To do so, use cell references to identify (point to) cells whose values you want to use in formulas.

When you double-tap a formula cell or open the formula keyboard, the table's *reference tabs* sprout letters and numbers that identify the columns and rows, respectively Ⓐ. Each *cell reference* is an address named for the column–row intersection where the cell is located. B2, for example, is the cell at the intersection of column B and row 2. A range of cells is identified by a pair of cell references separated by a colon (:). A1:B3, for example, refers to the rectangular block of six cells between A1 and B3 inclusive—that is, cells A1, A2, A3, B1, B2, and B3.

continues on next page

A cell reference in a formula tells Numbers to get that cell's value and use it in the formula's calculation. The simplest example is

=A1

which sets the value of the formula cell to whatever value is in cell A1. You can treat cell references like ordinary values. The formula

=A1 × 2

returns twice the value of A1, provided that A1 holds a number. **B** shows a formula that references multiple cells.

Cells also are referenced by name by using header-column and header-row values (see "Rows and Columns" in Chapter 2). If cell B4 has the header-column value Test 1 and the header-row value S333, its named reference is *Test 1 S333*.

Referenced cells can be in the same table as the formula cell, or they can be in another table on the same or a different sheet. Cell references have different formats, depending on whether they refer to a single cell or a range of cells, whether the cell's table has headers, and so on. **Table 4.4** lists the formats that Numbers uses for cell references.

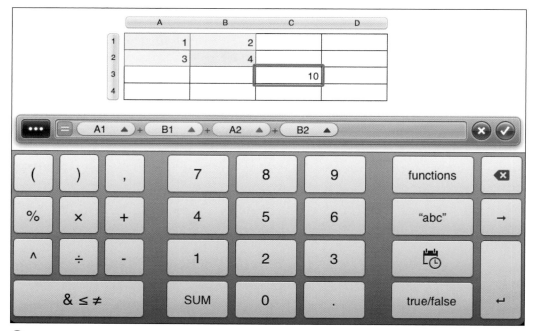

B Here, the formula cell, C3, sums the values in the four cells A1, B1, A2, and B2, which are temporarily color-coded to match the colors used in the formula bar. Formulas always reflect the current state of the spreadsheet. If you change any value in the range A1:B2, Numbers recalculates the result in C3 automatically.

TIP The first 26 columns of a table are labeled from A to Z. Column 27 is labeled AA, column 28 is AB, and so on. Cell BC500, for example, is located at the intersection of column 55 and row 500.

TIP For named references, Numbers omits the table or sheet name if the referenced cells have unique names in the spreadsheet.

TIP When referencing a cell in a table that has multiple header rows or columns, Numbers uses the name in the header cell *closest* to the referenced cell. For example, if a table has two header rows, and A1 contains XXX and A2 contains YYY, when you save a formula that uses a cell in column A, YYY is used in the named reference. (If YYY appears in another header cell in the spreadsheet, however, XXX is used).

TABLE 4.4 Cell Reference Formats

Referemce	Format	Example
A cell in the same table that contains the formula	The cell's reference tab letter (column) followed by its reference tab number (row)	*D3* refers to the third row in the fourth column.
A range of cells	A colon (:) between the first and last cell in the range, using reference tab notation	*D1:D4* refers to the first four cells in the fourth column.
All the cells in a column	The header-column name or the column letter	*D* refers to all the cells in the fourth column. *Test 2* refers to all the cells in the column whose header is Test 2.
All cells in a range of columns	A colon (:) between the header-column names or the letters of the first and last columns in the range	*C:D* refers to all the cells in the third and fourth columns. *Test 1:Test 4* refers to all the cells in the columns whose headers range from Test 1 to Test 4, inclusive.
All the cells in a row	The header-row name or row-number:row-number	*2:2* refers to all the cells in the second row. *S444* refers to all the cells in the row whose header is S444.
All cells in a range of rows	A colon (:) between the header-row names or the row numbers of the first and last rows in the range	*1:5* refers to all the cells in the first five rows. *S111:S444* refers to all the cells in the rows whose headers range from S111 to S444, inclusive.
A cell in a table that has a row header and a column header	The header-column name followed by the header-row name	*Test 2 S444* refers to a cell whose header row is S444 and whose header column is Test 2.
A cell in another table on the same sheet	The table name followed by two colons (::) and then the cell reference	*Table 2::C5* refers to cell C5 in the table named Table 2. *Test Scores::Test 2 S444* refers to a cell by name.
A cell in a table on another sheet	The sheet name followed by two colons (::), the table name, two colons (::), and then the cell reference	*Sheet 1::Table 2::C5* refers to cell C5 in the table named Table 2 on a sheet named Sheet 1. *Grades::Test Scores::Test 2 S444* refers to a cell by name.

Using Cell References

When you build a formula, you don't type the cell references yourself—Numbers inserts them for you when you select cells. A reference appears in the formula bar as a colored oval placeholder holding the name or reference-tab address of the cell(s). The color of each placeholder is coordinated to match the highlight color of the corresponding cells in the table **A**. You can easily redefine any cell reference in your formula **B**.

To insert a cell reference in a formula:

1. In the formula bar, position the insertion point where you want the reference to appear or, to replace an existing reference, tap its placeholder to select it.

2. Do any of the following:

   ▸ To refer to a single cell, tap the cell.

   ▸ To refer to a range of cells, touch and hold a cell in a corner of the range and drag across the range.

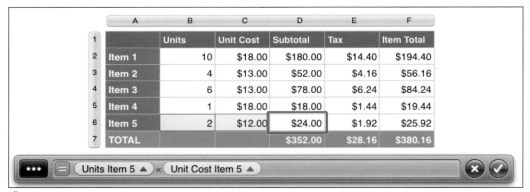

A Selecting a formula cell adds color highlights to its referenced cells in the table. Here, cell D6 references the two cells to its left. Color-matching makes it clear which cells you're using in the formula. Color highlighting appears only when you're editing a formula.

Selection handle

B Tap a cell reference in the formula bar to show selection handles in the corners of each block of referenced cells. To redefine a reference in the formula, drag the selection handles to expand or shrink the range, or drag the selection box itself to a new location.

- To refer to all the cells in a column, tap the column's letter on the reference tab. To refer to multiple columns, touch and hold a letter and drag left or right **C**.
- To refer to all the cells in a row, tap the row's number on the reference tab. To refer to multiple rows, touch and hold a number and drag up or down.
- To refer to cells in a different table on the same sheet, tap the target table and select a reference as described above.
- To refer to cells in a table on a different sheet, tap the sheet tab, tap the table, and then select a reference as described above.

Test Scores

	Student ID	Test 1	Test 2	Test 2	Test 4	Average
1						
2	S111	85	79	88	80	83
3	S222	92	95	91	100	94.5
4	S333	66	0	60	55	45.25
5	S444	71	77	78	80	76.5
6	S555	91	85	79	82	84.25
7	Average	81	67.2	79.2	79.4	76.7
8	Maximum	92	95	91	100	
9	Minimum	66	0	60	55	

AVERAGE (Test 1:Test 4 ▲)

C This multicolumn reference spans four columns (Test 1:Test 4). Header and footer cells are ignored when you select entire columns or rows, though you can redefine the range to include them.

Summing Values Quickly

To sum a column of values quickly, double-tap an empty cell at the bottom of the column, bring up the formula keyboard, and then tap the SUM key. Numbers auto-inserts the SUM function with a column reference.

Numbers makes it easy to use cell references to sum values. To create a formula that sums a bunch of cells, bring up the formula keyboard and start tapping cells. Numbers auto-inserts a + operator between each pair of references, creating a sum.

If the values to sum all occupy a block of neighboring cells, adding them is even easier: Bring up the formula keyboard and drag over the range of cells. Instead of using the + operator, Numbers uses the SUM function with a reference to your cell selection.

Understanding Comparison Operators

It's a common practice to base a formula's result on whether a certain condition is satisfied. The *comparison operators*, listed in **Table 4.5**, compare two values and evaluate to TRUE or FALSE (that is, to a Boolean value). The data type determines how values are compared:

- Numbers compare arithmetically. < means *smaller*, and > means *larger*. (To compare floating-point numbers for equality, use the DELTA function.)

- Text strings compare lexicographically. < means *precedes*, and > means *follows*. Text comparisons are case-insensitive. (To do a case-sensitive comparison, use the EXACT function.)

- Dates and times compare chronologically. < means *earlier*, and > means *later*. Date and times must have the same fields (year, month, day, hour, and so on) to be compared meaningfully.

- Durations compare by length. < means *shorter*, and > means *longer*.

- For Boolean values, TRUE > FALSE (and FALSE < TRUE) because TRUE is interpreted as 1 and FALSE is interpreted as 0.

It's usually a bad idea to compare values of different data types. Numbers typically flags such comparisons as errors, but there are a few situations where such comparisons are valid:

- Text strings compare greater than numbers. For example, "text" > 5, "5" > 5, and "" > 0 all return TRUE.

- Boolean values compare unequally to numbers. For example, TRUE = 1 and FALSE = 0 both return FALSE. TRUE ≠ 1 returns TRUE.

  Boolean values compare unequally to text strings. TRUE = "text" and FALSE = "FALSE" both return FALSE. TRUE ≠ "TRUE" returns TRUE.

TIP Comparison operators have lower precedence than arithmetic operators and functions. The expression SUM(A2, B2) + 5 > 10, for example, evaluates as ((SUM(A2, B2)) + 5) > 10. See also "Determining the Order of Operations" earlier in this chapter.

TIP The Checkbox format uses Boolean values. See "Editing and Formatting Cells" in Chapter 3.

TIP In Excel, comparison operators are called logical operators.

TABLE 4.5 Comparison Operators

Operator	Determines Whether	Example	Result
=	Two values are equal	ABC = abc	TRUE
≠	Two values are not equal	1 ≠ 1	FALSE
<	The first value is less than the second value	able < baker	TRUE
≤	The first value is less than or equal to the second value	1-Feb-2010 ≤ 1-Jan-2011	TRUE
>	The first value is greater than the second value	6 days > 1 week	FALSE
≥	The first value is greater than or equal to the second value	0 ≥ -1	TRUE

A This is the keypad for comparison operators. Tapping the bottommost key swaps in the keys for the arithmetic operators.

The & Operator

The & (ampersand) operator, visible in **A**, joins (concatenates) text strings. If A1 contains "aaa", B1 contains "bbb", and C1 contains "ccc", then the formula

`=A1 & B1 & C1`

returns "aaabbbccc".

You must add whitespace or delimiters (field separators) between the strings manually:

`=A1 & ", " & B1 & ", " & C1`

returns "aaa, bbb, ccc". The constant text values in the above formula are surrounded by quotation marks.

As an alternative to the & operator, you can use the CONCATENATE function.

Using Comparison Operators

You can use cell references or constants in comparisons. The expression A1=A2, for example, is TRUE if cell A1 contains the same value as cell A2. Comparison operations mainly are used in IF, AND, OR, NOT, SUMIF, COUNTIF, and other functions that take expressions that can be evaluated as TRUE or FALSE. For example, the formula

`=IF(B2=0, 0, B1/B2)`

uses a comparison to avoid dividing by zero.

Comparisons don't have to be embedded in functions; you can type them as stand-alone formulas. For example, the formula

`=A1=5`

will display TRUE or FALSE in a cell depending on the value in A1. Note that it's clearer to enter this formula as

`=(A1=5)`

To insert a comparison operator in a formula:

1. In the formula bar, position the insertion point where you want the operator to appear.

2. If the comparison-operator keys aren't visible on the left side of the formula keyboard, tap the &≤≠ key.

3. Tap an operator key **A**.

TIP You can use a numeric expression in place of a Boolean one. If the expression evaluates to 0, Numbers considers it to be **FALSE**; any other number is considered to be **TRUE**.

TIP When you sort rows based on a column that contains Boolean values, **TRUE** is interpreted as **1** and **FALSE** is interpreted as **0**. See "Sorting Rows in a Table" in Chapter 3.

Understanding Functions

You can do a lot by using only constants, operators, and cell references, but Numbers' real power comes from its *functions*: built-in, specialized, named operations that you can use in your formulas. Numbers gives you more than 250 functions, ranging from simple ones that sum or average numbers to complex ones that do financial and engineering calculations. See the appendix for a complete list of Numbers' functions.

In addition to working with numbers, functions can do calendar arithmetic, make logical decisions, search and transform text, and look up values in lists. **Table 4.6** lists some of the most commonly used functions.

Each function has a name followed by zero or more comma-separated arguments enclosed in parentheses. You use *arguments* to provide the values that the function needs to do its work. The CONVERT function, for example, takes a number in one measurement system and converts it to another system. Its *syntax*—which gives a function's name and the names and order of its arguments—is

CONVERT(*convert-num*, *from-unit*, *to-unit*)

Using CONVERT with sample arguments gives the formula

`=CONVERT(100, "C", "F")`

	A	B	C	D
1	convert-num	from-unit	to-unit	CONVERT
2	100	C	F	212
3	25	km	mi	15.534279805
4	32	F	C	0
5	100	km	m	100000
6	1	yr	wk	52.1775

Ⓐ The CONVERT functions in the last column get their arguments from the first three columns by using cell references.

TABLE 4.6 Commonly Used Functions

Function	Description
AND/OR/NOT	Creates a conditional formula that results in a Boolean value
AVERAGE	Calculates the arithmetic mean of a group of numbers
CONVERT	Converts a number from one measurement system to another system
COUNT	Counts the number of dates or numbers in a range
DATEDIF	Calculates the time difference between two dates
FIND/SEARCH	Finds one text string within another
IF	Creates a conditional formula that results in another calculation
INT	Rounds a number down to the nearest integer
ISERROR	Determines whether a value is an error
MIN/MAX	Returns the smallest/largest value of a group of numbers
NETWORKDAYS	Calculates the number of working days between two dates
NOW	Returns the current date and time
NPV	Calculate the net present value of an investment
RAND	Returns a uniform random number between 0 and 1
REPLACE/ SUBSTITUTE	Replaces one text string with another
ROUND	Rounds a number to the specified number of decimal places
SQRT	Returns the square root of a number
SUM	Calculates the sum of a group of numbers
TRIM	Removes extra spaces from text
UPPER/LOWER/ PROPER	Changes the case of text
VALUE	Converts text to a number
VLOOKUP/ HLOOKUP/ LOOKUP	Looks up values in a list

This formula displays 212 in a cell—100 degrees Celsius expressed in the Fahrenheit scale, and

`=CONVERT(25, "km", "mi")`

displays the number of miles in 25 kilometers (15.53427...) **Ⓐ**.

The number and types of arguments vary by function. You can type arguments directly into the formula or use cell references for some or all arguments. Arguments can be constants, operator expressions, cell references, or other functions. Text arguments must go inside quotation marks (but don't put cell references inside quotation marks—they aren't considered to be text even if their cells contain text). Here are a few examples of valid arguments:

`=CONVERT(60+40, "C", "F")`

`=CONVERT(A2, B2, C2)`

`=CONVERT(A2+10, B2, UPPER("f"))`

`=CONVERT(SUM(D2:D10)+SUM(F2:F10)-273.15, B2, UPPER(LEFT("fahrenheit",1)))`

Functions that take no arguments need no user-supplied data to do their work. The TODAY function, for example, returns today's date:

`=TODAY()`

continues on next page

TIP Functions have higher precedence than arithmetic operators and comparison operators. The expression SUM(A2, B2) + 5 > 10, for example, evaluates as ((SUM(A2, B2)) + 5) > 10. See also "Determining the Order of Operations" earlier in this chapter.

TIP You can't create custom functions in Numbers as you can in Excel. Numbers has no equivalent of Visual Basic for Applications (VBA).

Optional Arguments

Some functions take *optional arguments*. If you omit an optional argument from the function, Numbers uses a *default value* when it evaluates the function. If you want to use a value other than the default, specify an optional argument just as you would a required one. The LOG function, for example, returns the logarithm of a positive number by using a specified base. LOG has two arguments:

LOG(*pos-num*, *base*)

The first argument is required; the second is optional. (Optional arguments, if they exist, always follow required ones.) If you omit *base*, it is assumed to be 10. Hence

=LOG(100)

is the same as

=LOG(100,10)

A function's help window tells you whether an argument is required or optional and, for the latter, gives its default value. If you omit some optional arguments but not others, don't delete the commas between them.

Using Functions

A function can be one of several elements in a formula, or it can be the only element in a formula. When you build a formula, you don't type the function names yourself—you use the *function browser* to insert them. The function browser lets you flick through Numbers' entire library of functions. When you find the function you want, Numbers inserts it into your formula, including gray-oval argument placeholders. Placeholders for optional arguments are a lighter gray than those of required arguments.

To insert a function in a formula:

1. In the formula bar, position the insertion point where you want the function to appear or, to replace an existing function, tap its name to select it.

2. Tap the functions key on the keyboard and do one of the following:

   ▸ To access all Numbers' functions, tap Categories, tap a category, and then tap a function **A**. (To see every function, tap the All category.)

   ▸ To access a function that you've used recently, tap Recent and tap a function **B**.

   continues on next page

continues on next page

A Don't let the category names intimidate you. The Statistical category contains such commonplace functions as AVERAGE and COUNT, Engineering includes CONVERT, and Numeric has SUM.

B Each time you use a function, Numbers inserts it at the top of the Recent list and removes the least recently used (bottommost) function.

- To get help with a function, tap 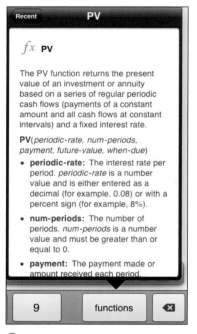 next to its name **C**. After you finish reading, tap the back button in the top-left corner of the help window to return to the list of functions, and then tap a function.

Numbers inserts the function and its arguments placeholders in the formula bar.

3. In the formula bar, tap each argument placeholder and do one of the following **D** and **E**:

  - To insert a cell reference, tap a cell or drag across a cell range.

  - To insert a nested function, tap the functions key.

  - To insert an arithmetic or comparison operator, tap an operator key on the formula keyboard. To switch between the operators, tap the &≤≠ or ()+÷ key.

  - To insert a number, tap the number keys on the formula keyboard.

  - To insert text, tap the "abc" key.

Recent   **PV**

fx **PV**

The PV function returns the present value of an investment or annuity based on a series of regular periodic cash flows (payments of a constant amount and all cash flows at constant intervals) and a fixed interest rate.

PV(*periodic-rate, num-periods, payment, future-value, when-due*)

- **periodic-rate:** The interest rate per period. *periodic-rate* is a number value and is either entered as a decimal (for example, 0.08) or with a percent sign (for example, 8%).

- **num-periods:** The number of periods. *num-periods* is a number value and must be greater than or equal to 0.

- **payment:** The payment made or amount received each period.

  9   functions   ⌫

C A help window includes a function's name, purpose, and syntax, as well as descriptions of arguments, usage notes, examples, and links to related functions.

•••   = (PV (*periodic-rate*), (*num-periods*), (*payment*), (*future-value*), (*when-due* ▲)) ✖ ✔

D The placeholder of the selected argument is highlighted in blue. The last two arguments are optional, indicated by the lighter color of their placeholders.

	A	B	C	D	E	F
1	periodic-rate	num-periods	payment	future-value	when-due	PV
2	0.2500%	180	($100.00)	$100000.00		($49318.08)
3	0.2500%	180	($100.00)	$100000.00	1	($49318.08)
4	0.2500%	180	($200.00)	$100000.00	0	($34837.54)
5	0.2500%	180	($200.00)	$100000.00	1	($34837.54)

•••   = (PV (A2 ▲), (B2 ▲), (C2 ▲), (D2 ▲), (when-due ▲)) ✖ ✔

E The arguments in this function (cell F2) all are cell references, except for the last argument, which is optional and, here, omitted.

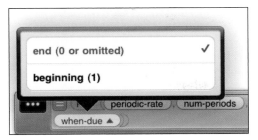

 Tap a menu entry to fill in the argument, or tap off the menu to leave the argument unchanged.

- To insert a date, time, or duration, tap the 📅 key.
- To insert a Boolean value, tap the true/false key.
- To omit an optional argument, leave its placeholder as is. Or, to delete the placeholder, tap the placeholder to select it, tap it again, and then tap Cut in the pop-up menu.

TIP If an argument takes only a limited number of discrete values, its placeholder will show a triangle. You can tap this triangle for a pop-up menu of choices 🅵.

TIP To open the help window of a function within the formula bar, tap the function name to select it, and then tap the name again.

TIP The help windows for every function are collected in the iWork Formulas and Functions User Guide, available for download in PDF format at support.apple.com/manuals/#iwork. (Numbers for iPad uses a large subset of Numbers for Mac functions.)

Copying and Moving Formulas

When you copy or move numbers, text, or other raw values, Numbers duplicates the value in the target cells. Copying and moving formulas, however, is complicated by cell references, which you may not want to duplicate. Numbers' default behavior is what you want most of the time:

- When you *move* a formula cell, Numbers leaves its original cell references untouched; in its new location, the formula still points to the same cells that it used to **A** and **B**.

- When you *copy* a formula cell, Numbers updates the formula's cell references so that they point to different cells *relative* to the formula's new location **C**.

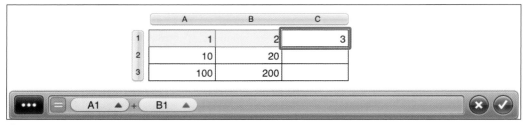

A The original formula, in cell C1, sums cells A1 and B1.

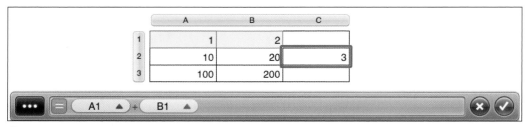

B When you *move* C1 to C2, the cell references don't change: the formula still sums A1 and B1.

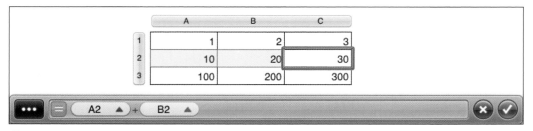

C When you *copy* C1 to C2 and C3, the cell references change: Each copied formula sums the two cells to its left—the same relative position of the referenced cells in the original formula.

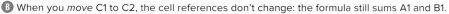

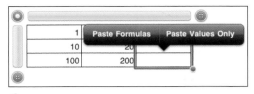

D When you paste a formula, tap Paste Formulas. Tapping Paste Values Only pastes the *result* of the formula but not the actual formula—which is handy when you have a result that you no longer want to update.

You can move formulas by dragging. You can copy formulas by cut-and-paste, copy-and-paste, or filling **D**. These techniques are covered in "Copying and Moving Cells" and "Filling Cells with Data Series" in Chapter 3. You might think that cut-and-paste moves a cell, but it actually copies it—it only *looks* moved because its contents disappear from its original location. Numbers considers all pasted cells to be copies of the original. Still, it's common to refer to cutting-and-pasting as moving (particularly when dealing with raw values rather than formulas).

By default, cell addresses in formulas are *relative cell references*, meaning their row or column addresses can change when you copy formulas (refer to **C**). For situations where you want to *preserve* row or column positions, Numbers offers *absolute cell references*, which freeze cell addresses no matter where you copy formula cells.

TIP To copy the *text* of a formula, double-tap an empty area of the formula bar and tap Select All in the pop-up menu. (To copy only part of the text, drag the blue drag points to encompass the characters that you want to copy.) Tap Copy in the pop-up menu. When you paste the formula's text in a new cell, all the cell references stay the same as they were in the original.

To set relative and absolute cell references:

1. In the formula bar, tap the triangle in the placeholder of the cell reference that you want to preserve.

2. Slide Preserve Row or Preserve Column to ON (absolute) or OFF (relative) for the beginning or end addresses of the selected range **E**. A $ character in the cell reference indicates an absolute row or column:

   Relative column–relative row (A1). When the formula cell is copied, the cell reference changes so that it retains the same position relative to the formula cell (refer to **C**).

   Absolute column–absolute row (A1). When the formula cell is copied, the cell reference doesn't change **F**.

   Relative column–absolute row (A$1). When the formula cell is copied, only the column component can change to retain its position relative to the formula cell.

   Absolute column–relative row ($A1). When the formula cell is copied, only the row component can change to retain its position relative to the formula cell.

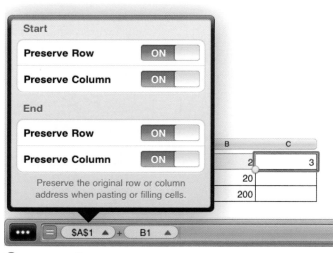

E Here, as in **A**, the formula in cell C1 sums cells A1 and B1, but this formula uses the absolute cell reference A1. The B1 reference still is relative.

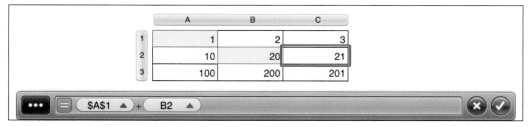

F When copying the formula, as in **C**, the B1 reference changes to B2, but A1 stays anchored.

Handling Errors

When a formula cell contains an error, Numbers displays a red triangle in the middle of the cell. Double-tap the cell to see the error message and fix the formula **A**. Some common errors are:

- Invalid cell references.

- Syntax errors: Including unpaired parentheses, misplacing operators (2xx2), or including too many or too few function arguments (count the commas).

- Math errors: Dividing by zero, taking the square root of a negative number, or taking the log of a nonpositive number.

- Domain errors: Comparing values with incompatible data types (2 < FALSE) or doing arithmetic on non-numbers (2 + "text").

- Circular references: Creating a formula that depends, indirectly or directly, on its own value.

- Overflows: Calculating numbers that are too big for Numbers to handle (9999^9999).

TIP Formulas that reference cells with errors are themselves flagged as errors, possibly causing a ripple effect that fills your table with red triangles. Unfortunately, Numbers for iPad lacks the auditing tools of Excel or Numbers for Mac, so you'll have to hunt for seminal bad cells. The **ISERROR** and **IFERROR** functions are useful for preventing cascading errors.

A Fortunately, errors that trigger the vaguely worded "The formula contains a syntax error" usually are easy to fix. An extra parenthesis dangling at the end of this formula caused a syntax error.

5

Charts

Trends and comparisons are hard to discern from raw data, so Numbers provides charts to reveal relationships that aren't apparent by staring at rows and columns of numbers. You can choose from many types of charts—bar charts, pie charts, scatter charts, and more—and you have many ways to customize and embellish them. Knowing which chart type to pick isn't always easy, and decorating charts with *chartjunk*—unnecessary text, lines, shading, effects, and doodads—is the path to the dark side.

This chapter contains advice on choosing, creating, and formatting charts for particular types of data, but the art and science of charting is a big topic that's beyond the scope of this book. If you're inclined, one of the best books on the subject is scholarly, minimalist, thought-provoking, and acerbic: Edward Tufte's *The Visual Display of Quantitative Information, Second Edition* (Graphics Press, 2001).

In This Chapter

Chart Basics

When you add a chart to your spreadsheet, Numbers puts a *placeholder chart* on the current sheet, preloaded with sample (fake) data. You can use the sample column chart to learn the basic features of charts Ⓐ. Numbers for iPad uses the same chart terms as Excel and Numbers for Mac.

Source table. A *source table* contains the data to graph. A source table doesn't actually appear alongside a placeholder chart, but I've recreated one here to illustrate the concept. The chart shows whatever data is selected in the source table; you can select all the table's cells (as shown in Ⓐ) or only some of them Ⓑ. (You even can select only one cell, which wouldn't tell much of a story.) A chart is linked dynamically to its source table—when you change a cell's value or select a different range of cells, the associated chart updates automatically. Tables and charts aren't monogamous: A table can feed data to multiple charts, and a chart can get data from more than one table.

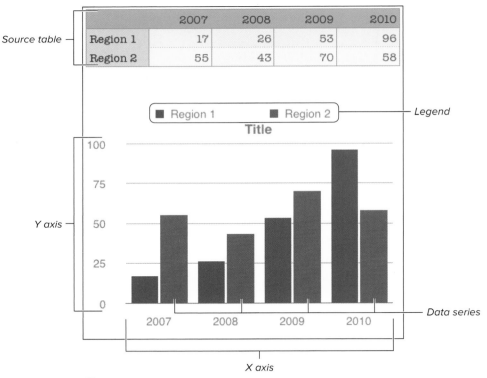

Ⓐ The placeholder column chart plots two data series, Region 1 and Region 2, over four years.

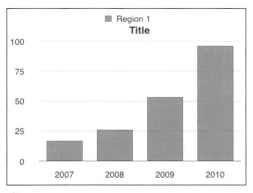

B This column chart, which references only the first two rows of the source table, plots one data series, Region 1, over four years.

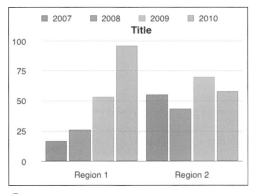

C This column chart contains two sets of four columns (eight data points). The data points for each *year* are data series (each series has only two data points) and each *region* is a category.

Data points and data series. Here, the source table has eight *data points* (values)—four for each region. In the chart, Region 1 and Region 2 are called the *data series* because each region's data points appear as a series of columns of the same color, one column for each year. Each Region 1 column is paired beside its corresponding Region 2 column, and each side-by-side set of columns is called a *data set* or *category* (2007 is a category, 2008 is a category, and so on). Numbers lets you transpose data series to change the emphasis of your data. Here, for example, you can group data points by region rather than by year **C**.

Legend. The *legend* shows the colors, symbols, and labels used for each data series in the chart. The legend's labels come from the headers of the rows or columns containing the data series (for details about headers, see "Rows and Columns" in Chapter 2). You can show or hide the legend.

X axis and y axis. The *x axis* and the *y axis* are the horizontal and vertical lines that give a chart scale and context. In column, bar, area, and line charts, data points are plotted on one axis (the y axis for column, area, and line charts; the x axis for bar charts) and categories are grouped on the other axis. The data-point (numeric) axis is called the *value axis*, and the data-set (group) axis is called the *category axis*. In scatter charts, both the x and y axes are value axes. Pie charts have no axes. Category axes are labeled with text from row or column headers in the source table; value axes are labeled with a numeric range. Axes are marked by stepped graduations called *tick marks* and *gridlines*, which you can show, hide, reformat, and (on value axes) rescale.

Choosing a Chart Type

Numbers offers nine different chart types, each of which is designed for certain situations or data types .

Column. Column charts display vertical columns with lengths proportional to the values that they represent. They're often used to compare groups over time (**B** and **C**) or rank discrete things by some numeric measure (country on the x axis and population on the y axis, for example).

A Each chart type has its strengths and weaknesses for different types of data. Helpfully, Numbers doesn't offer 3D chart styles—the crowning accomplishment of chartjunk.

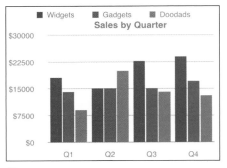

B This column chart compares sales of three products over a year.

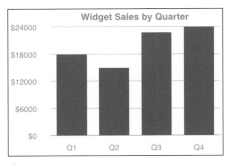

C This column chart shows the sales trend of a single product over time. A line chart might be a better choice here.

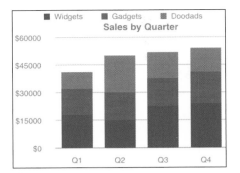

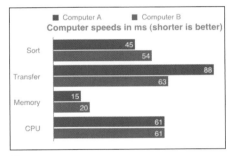

D This stacked column chart uses the same data as **B**, but shows the combined sales of all three products over time. It's usually a bad idea to try to estimate or compare the individual values (different colors) within the columns of this type of chart.

E This bar chart compares the time that it takes two computers to complete four different tasks. Bar charts look best when you hide the x-axis and display the values at the end of each bar.

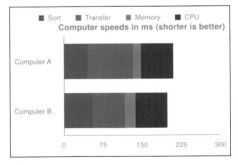

F This stacked bar chart uses the same data as **E** but combines the results of all four time trials end-to-end.

Stacked Column. Stacked column charts display the results of multiple data series, combined and stacked atop one another like towers of blocks. These charts use the same data as regular column charts but emphasize overall effects rather than individual values **D**.

Bar. Bar charts are column charts turned sideways (that is, with their axes swapped). They're often used to compare the speed or duration of events **E**.

Stacked Bar. Stacked bar charts are like stacked column charts, only sideways, and with the same caveats **F**.

continues on next page

Line. Line charts display data series as points connected by straight line segments. They're often used to show trends over time. If you've got a lot of points to plot, line charts are a cleaner and more compact alternative to column charts **G**.

Area. Area charts are like line charts but fill in the space below each line (data series) with a different color. Like line charts, they're often used to show trends over time **H**.

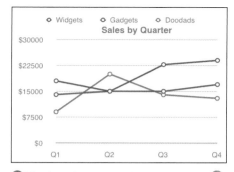

G This line chart shows the same data as **B**. Try to limit line charts to five lines (data series) or fewer, lest you end up with a spaghetti chart.

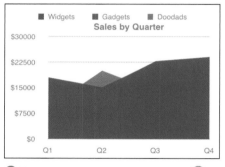

H This area chart uses the same data as **B**. Comparing it to the line chart **G** shows the chief danger of area charts: Data series that cross can disappear behind each other— here, most Doodads and all Gadgets values are invisible. Area charts violate the chartjunk principle of putting as little ink on the page as possible.

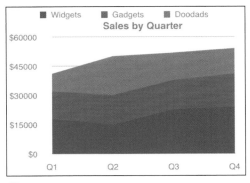

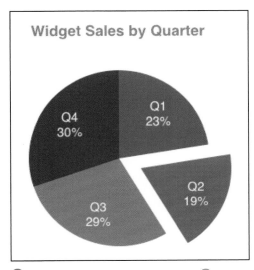

Sales by Quarter

Widget Sales by Quarter

I This stacked area chart uses the same data as B but shows the combined sales of all three products over time. Unlike regular area charts, stacked area charts pose no danger of hidden data points.

J The pie chart uses the same data as C but shows each quarter's widget sales as a proportion of the entire year. You can drag slices out of the pie to emphasize them. Note how much harder it is to see the difference between Q3 and Q4 (or even Q1 and Q2) in the pie chart than in the column chart.

Stacked Area. Like stacked column and bar charts, stacked area charts emphasize overall effects rather than individual values. The continuous color and joined line segments "flow" rightward across the chart, so they're better than stacked column charts for comparing groups over time I.

Pie. A pie chart is a circle divided into slices, with each slice showing a percentage of the whole. (Technically, the arc length of each sector of the circle—and consequently its area—is proportional to the value it represents.) Pies show proportions, not specific data values, so they work best for graphing a single row or column with few cells. Pie charts are like movie stepchildren: loved but secretly evil. It's hard to compare different slices of a pie, particularly those with similar values (and forget about comparing data across different pies) J. They're not bad if you want to compare the size of a single slice to the whole pie, but you're almost always better off with a single-series column chart, or even a non-graphical table of values.

Scatter. A scatter chart (also called a scatterplot and adored by scientists and statisticians) displays data differently from the other types of charts: It plots every data point on its own x and y coordinates. A scatter chart has two value axes and needs at least two columns or rows of continuous numeric data to plot values for a single data series. To show multiple data series, you use additional two-column (or two-row) pairs. Each pair of data values determines the position of one data point:

The first value determines the point's position on the x-axis, and the second determines its position on the y-axis. Because scatter charts have no category axis, don't convert other types of charts (which don't use paired, or *bivariate*, data) to scatter charts, or vice versa **K**.

TIP Unlike Excel and Numbers for Mac, Numbers for iPad doesn't support mixed charts, which display multiple data series in two or more chart styles.

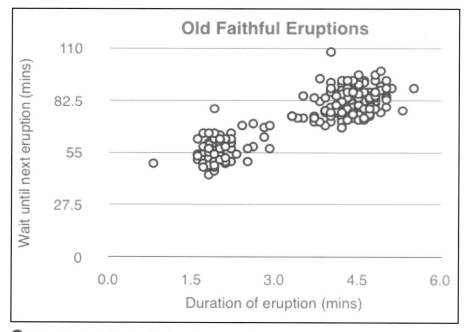

K This scatter chart plots the duration of an eruption (x axis) against the waiting time until the next eruption (y axis) for the Old Faithful geyser in Yellowstone National Park, Wyoming, USA. It looks like eruptions come mostly in two flavors: short-wait-short-duration and long-wait-long-duration. Many versions of this dataset are floating around; my source is S. Chatterjee, *et al.*, *A Casebook for a First Course in Statistics and Data Analysis* (Wiley, 1994).

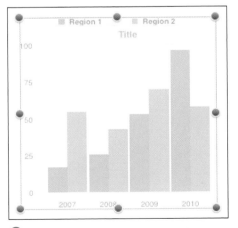

A Flick left or right in this window to see all the colors for each chart type.

B A freshly added placeholder chart keeps its faded appearance until you link it to a table.

Creating a Chart

A chart can show all the data in a table or data only in selected cells of one or more tables. You can add, delete, and edit a chart's data series at any time. If a table has header rows or header columns, Numbers uses the header text as axis and legend labels (for header details, see "Rows and Columns" in Chapter 2).

To add a chart:

1. Tap in the toolbar, and then tap Charts **A**.

2. Tap the type and color scheme of chart that you want to add.

   A placeholder chart appears on the current sheet **B**.

3. Do any of the following:

   ▸ To move the chart, drag it.

   ▸ To resize the chart, drag one of the blue selection handles on the chart's perimeter (if the handles aren't visible, tap the chart).

   ▸ To layer the chart above or below other objects on the sheet, tap **i** in the toolbar, tap Arrange, and then drag the Back/Front slider.

To link a chart to a table:

1. Double-tap the chart 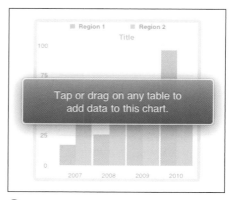.

2. Touch and hold your fingertip on any table, and then tap and drag to select data series **D**.

   The chart updates instantly as you change the selection. You can select multiple ranges within a table or across multiple tables.

3. Tap Done in the top-right corner of the window.

TIP Deleting a table severs any links that it has to charts, which then revert to placeholder charts.

C This pop-up tip appears when a chart is ready to be linked to a table.

Selection handle

	Q1	Q2	Q3	Q4
Widgets	$18000	$15000	$22750	$24000
Gadgets	$14000	$15000	$15000	$17000
Doodads	$9000	$20000	$14000	$13000

	Q1	Q2	Q3	Q4
Widgets	$18000	$15000	$22750	$24000
Gadgets	$14000	$15000	$15000	$17000
Doodads	$9000	$20000	$14000	$13000

	Q1	Q2	Q3	Q4
Widgets	$18000	$15000	$22750	$24000
Gadgets	$14000	$15000	$15000	$17000
Doodads	$9000	$20000	$14000	$13000

	Q1	Q2	Q3	Q4
Widgets	$18000	$15000	$22750	$24000
Gadgets	$14000	$15000	$15000	$17000
Doodads	$9000	$20000	$14000	$13000

D This part takes practice. These figures show samples of selected contiguous and noncontiguous row and column series. The easiest way to select a data series is to tap its row or column header, but you can select any range by touching and holding a cell and dragging. If you end up with a mess of ranges and purple selection handles, you can backtrack by deleting one series at a time, or bail out completely by tapping Done and then Undo.

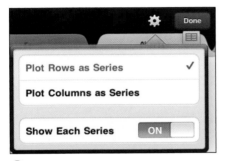

	Q1	Q2	Q3	Q4
Delete Series ts	$18000	$15000	$22750	$24000
Gadgets	$14000	$15000	$15000	$17000
Doodads	$9000	$20000	$14000	$13000

	Q1	Q2	Q3	Q4
Widgets	$18000	$15000	$22750	$24000
Gadgets	$14000	$15000	$15000	$17000
Doodads	$9000	$20000	$14000	$13000

E Here, the entire table is selected (top). Deleting the Gadgets data series leaves two noncontiguous ranges: Widgets and Doodads (bottom).

⚙	Done
Plot Rows as Series	✓
Plot Columns as Series	
Show Each Series	ON

F The Plot commands work best if your data series span entire rows or columns.

To edit data series:

1. Double-tap the chart.

2. In the linked table, do any of the following:

   ▸ To delete a series, tap the dark handle adjacent to the series, and then tap Delete Series **E**.

   ▸ To add a series, touch and hold a cell and drag across a range, or tap a header cell to add an entire row or column.

   ▸ To swap rows and columns as series, tap ⚙ in the top-right corner of the screen, and then tap your preference **F**.

   ▸ To resize series individually, tap ⚙, slide Show Each Series to ON (refer to **F**), and then drag the purple selection handles to encompass the desired range **G**.

3. Tap Done in the top-right corner of the window.

TIP Charts ⊞ When you're editing a chart, a small table icon appears on the tab of each sheet that holds a table linked to the chart.

	Q1	Q2	Q3	Q4
Widgets	$18000	$15000	$22750	$24000
Gadgets	$14000	$15000	$15000	$17000
Doodads	$9000	$20000	$14000	$13000

	Q1	Q2	Q3	Q4
Widgets	$18000	$15000	$22750	$24000
Gadgets	$14000	$15000	$15000	$17000
Doodads	$9000	$20000	$14000	$13000

G When Show Each Series is OFF, Numbers shows contiguous data series with a single selection handle, so they can be resized as a group (left). Turning Show Each Series ON gives each series its own selection handle, for individual control (right).

To cut, copy, or delete a chart:

1. Tap the chart to select it, tap it again, and then tap Cut, Copy, or Delete in the pop-up menu 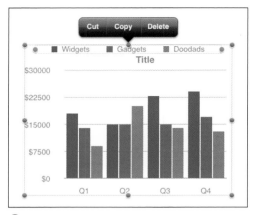.

2. To paste a cut or copied chart, go to the destination (which can be in a different sheet), tap an empty area on the sheet, and then tap Paste in the pop-up menu.

   Pasted charts within the same spread-sheet still reference their original tables.

TIP If you paste a chart into a different spreadsheet file, Numbers severs the chart's links to the original table and pastes a new source table along with the chart. This table contains a copy of all the chart's original data series. If the chart referenced multiple tables, all the original tables' data series are consolidated in the new table.

TIP You can paste charts from Numbers into Pages and Keynote documents.

H Cut removes the chart so that it can be moved (pasted) elsewhere. Copy copies a chart so that it can be duplicated (pasted) elsewhere, leaving the original chart. Delete removes the chart (without placing a copy on the clipboard).

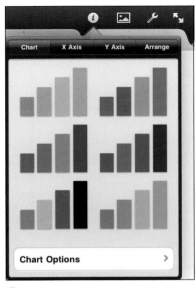

A The colors are preset to match the template you're using.

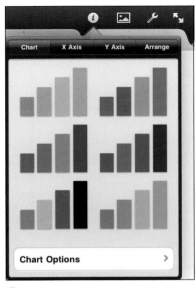

B If you want to see what the same data look like charted in different ways, tap Chart Type. You can always come back to your original type.

Formatting a Chart

You can change a chart's type, color scheme, fonts, text size, numeric formats, title, labels, gridlines, tick marks, and much more. Experiment to learn the effects of the options: Change them and watch how the chart updates. And remember the chart purist's mantra: minimalism, clarity, restraint.

To format a chart:

1. Tap the chart to select it.
2. Tap **ⓘ** in the toolbar.
3. Do any of the following:
   - ▸ To change the chart's color scheme, tap Chart and tap the look you want **A**.
   - ▸ To change the type of chart, tap Chart > Chart Options > Chart Type. See "Choosing a Chart Type" earlier in this chapter.
   - ▸ To change the font and text size, and to show or hide the title, legend, border, and value labels, tap Chart > Chart Options **B**.

continues on next page

▸ To show, hide, or edit axis lines, labels, and markings, tap X Axis or Y Axis **C**.

TIP Flick up and down the **ⓘ** window to see all the chart options.

TIP To edit a chart title or axis title, double-tap it and enter a new title by using the usual text selection and editing commands (see "Editing and Formatting Cells" in Chapter 3). You may need to zoom in on the chart to double-tap an axis label accurately.

C The options for a value axis let you rescale the chart manually. Tap Value Scale Settings to set the minimum and maximum values of the axis. If your data values are all positive and spread over a very large range (orders of magnitude), try turning on the Log (logarithmic transformation) option to tighten the range and induce symmetry.

Text Boxes, Shapes, and Images

You can adorn your spreadsheets with:

- Text boxes
- Lines
- Arrows
- Geometric shapes
- Photos
- Movies

Text boxes are useful for adding titles and annotations, and arrows can point out notable results. As for the other objects, let's just say that even Apple had a hard time finding a legitimate use for them with Numbers' built-in spreadsheet templates (stock nature photos on the Travel Planner, for example). Nevertheless, you've got 'em if you want 'em, just as you do in the other iWork apps, Pages and Keynote (where they *are* useful).

Creating an Object

An object is any item that you add to a spreadsheet and can manipulate. Tables and charts are objects, as are text boxes, lines, arrows, shapes, images, and movies.

To add a text box, line, arrow, or shape:

1. Tap ⊡ in the toolbar, and then tap Shapes **A**.

2. Do one of the following:

   ▸ To add a text box, tap the **T** icon.

   ▸ To add one of the other objects, tap its icon.

   Alternatively, touch and hold an icon and drag it to the sheet.

3. To reposition the object, drag it.

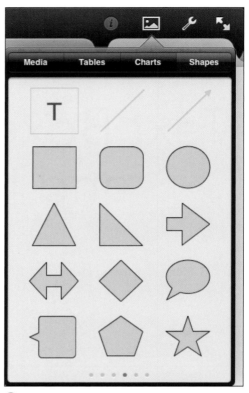

A The colors and border styles are preset to match the template you're using. Flick left or right to see all the options.

B Tap an album to see its images. To backtrack, tap the back arrow at the top of the window.

To add an image or movie:

1. Tap 🖼 in the toolbar, and then tap Media **B**.

2. Do one of the following:

   ▸ To add an image, tap its album, and then tap the image.

   ▸ To add a movie, tap its thumbnail image, and then tap Use.

   Alternatively, touch and hold an image and drag it to the sheet.

3. To reposition the object, drag it.

TIP **Synchronizing with iTunes is covered in the** *iPad User Guide*. **To read it, tap the bookmark in Safari or go to help.apple.com/ipad.**

Photos and Movies

All objects except images and movies are built in to Numbers. To sync sync photos with your computer, use iTunes. To import photos directly from a digital camera, iPhone, iPod touch, or SD memory card, use Apple's iPad Camera Connection Kit. iPad and Numbers support standard photo formats: JPEG, TIFF, GIF, and PNG. You can export movies from video-editing software (such as iMovie or Windows Live Movie Maker) to iTunes in M4V, MP4, or MOV format. Once in iTunes, movies can be synced to your iPad.

Working with Images

After adding an image, you can replace it with a different image or mask it to hide or zoom parts of it. For other tasks, see "Styling Objects" and "Arranging Objects" later in this chapter.

To replace an image:

1. If it's a placeholder image, tap 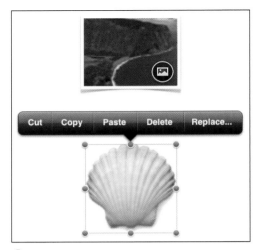 at the bottom of the image placeholder **A**.

   or

   If it's an existing image, tap the image to select it, tap it again, and then tap Replace in the pop-up menu.

2. In the Photo Albums window, tap an album, and then tap the replacement image.

   The image appears within a mask, so it may be cropped (to fix it, see below).

3. Tap anywhere outside the image.

To mask an image:

1. Double-tap the image.

   The image mask appears **B**.

2. Do any of the following:

   ▸ To resize the image within the mask, drag the slider below the image.

   ▸ To resize the mask, drag the blue selection handles on the mask's perimeter.

   ▸ To change the part of the image that's visible within the mask, drag the image.

   ▸ To restore the original mask, tap **ℹ** > Arrange > Reset Mask.

3. When you're finished, tap Done or tap anywhere outside the image.

A Some of the images that come with the built-in templates are placeholder images (top), which sport a 🖻 badge for quick access to the Photo Albums window. For other images (bottom), you must use the editing menu.

Selection handle

B An image's mask determines which part of the picture is visible. Changing the mask doesn't edit or permanently crop the image.

A The paragraph styles (Title, Subtitle, and so on) are preset to match the template you're using. Flick up or down to see them all.

> **Every time a friend succeeds, I die a little.**
> —*Gore Vidal*
>
> **Distress, n. A disease incurred by exposure to the prosperity of a friend.**
> —*Ambrose Bierce*

B The quotations in this text box have the Heading style applied; the author names use the Label Dark style.

Formatting Text

After adding a text box or shape, you can double-tap it to add text. Use the same text-selection and editing techniques described in "Editing and Formatting Cells" in Chapter 3. You can format selected text by applying preset paragraph styles or by customizing the font, typeface, size, color, alignment, and other attributes.

To apply a paragraph style:

To apply a single paragraph style to all the text, tap the text box or shape to select it. Tap **ⓘ**, tap Text, and then tap a paragraph style.

or

To apply a paragraph style to only some paragraphs, double-tap the text box or shape, and then select the target paragraph(s). Tap **ⓘ**, tap Style, and then tap a paragraph style **A** and **B**.

TIP Paragraph styles apply to *entire* paragraphs. Even if you select only a portion of text within a paragraph, the whole paragraph is restyled. If you're applying a style to only one paragraph, just tap so the blinking insertion point appears anywhere in the paragraph, and then tap a style.

TIP You cannot rename or edit the built-in paragraph styles or create new ones.

To change the typeface:

1. Double-tap the text box or shape and select the target text.

2. Tap , tap Style, and then tap a typeface button to apply bold, italic, underline, or strikethrough C and D.

TIP To select a word, double-tap it. To select a paragraph, triple-tap it.

C You can turn the typeface buttons on and off independently to...

Bold
Italic
Underline
~~Strikethrough~~
All of the above

D ...apply any combination of typefaces.

To create bulleted, lettered, or numbered lists:

1. Double-tap the text box or shape and select the target paragraphs.

2. Tap 🅘, tap List, and then tap the list type.

3. Tap the arrows at the top of the window to indent or un-indent list items 🄴 and 🄵.

🄴 Numbers and letters auto-increment for each new paragraph.

- Bulleted list
- Bulleted list
  1. Numbered sublist
  2. Numbered sublist
     A. Lettered sub-sublist
     B. Lettered sub-sublist
- Bulleted list

🄵 Using different list styles for each indent level shows the hierarchy of information clearly.

To change the font size, text color, or font:

1. Double-tap the text box or shape and select the target text.

2. Tap ⓘ, tap Style, flick to the bottom of the window, and then tap Text Options ⓖ and ⓗ.

3. Do any of the following:

   ▸ To set the font size, tap the up or down Size arrows.

   ▸ To set the text color, tap the Color swatch, flick left or right to see all the colors, and then tap the color you want. To return to the other options, tap ◀.

   ▸ To set the font, tap Font, flick up or down to see all the fonts, and then tap the font you want. To choose a typeface, tap ❯ on the right side of the font name. To return to the other options, tap ◀.

TIP Text boxes (but not shapes) grow auto-matically to show all their text. If an object is too small to display all the text that it contains, a ⊞ appears on the object's border ⓘ.

ⓖ Fonts will display and print clearly at any size.

36-Point Green Helvetica Bold Oblique

ⓗ For some fonts, the Font menu offers more typeface variations than are available on the Style menu (refer to ⓒ).

36-Point Green Helvetica Bold

ⓘ This text box contains *overset* text, meaning some text isn't visible. Possible fixes: Increase the size of the text box, decrease the font size, delete some text, or increase the number of columns.

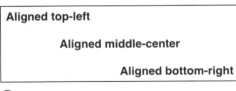

J Inset Margin and Columns apply to all the text in the object, even if only some text is selected. Alignment and Line Spacing apply to selected paragraphs only.

Aligned top-left
Aligned middle-center
Aligned bottom-right

K Multiple alignments. 8-point inset. One column. Double line spacing.

To change the alignment, inset margin, number of columns, and line spacing:

1. Double-tap the text box or shape and select the target text.
2. Tap **i** and then tap Layout **J** and **K**.
3. Do any of the following:
   - ▸ Tap the Alignment buttons on the left to align text horizontally: left, center, right, or justified. The Alignment buttons on the right align text vertically: top, middle, or bottom. (This setting applies to selected paragraphs only.)
   - ▸ Slide the Inset Margin slider to set the distance between the text and the edge of the object's border, in points. (This setting applies to all the object's text.)
   - ▸ Tap a Columns button (1–4) to set the number of columns into which the text flows. (This setting applies to all the object's text.)
   - ▸ Tap the up and down Line Spacing arrows to set the amount of whitespace between lines. (This setting applies to selected paragraphs only.)

continues on next page

TIP To apply object-wide settings quickly: Tap a text box or shape to select it and then tap **ⓘ** > **Text** > **Text Options ⓛ**.

To copy and paste a text style:

1. Double-tap the text box or shape containing the text whose style you want to copy.

2. Select the text and tap More > Copy Style in the pop-up menu **Ⓜ**.

3. Select another range of text within your spreadsheet.

4. Tap More > Paste Style.

ⓛ The Text Options window applies settings to all an object's text in one shot.

Ⓜ A faster alternative to slogging repeatedly through style windows is to copy only the style from a bit of text and then paste (apply) that style to other text within your spreadsheet.

Web Addresses in Text

When you type or paste a web address in a text box or shape, Numbers recognizes it and autoformats it as an underlined blue hyperlink. To open the link's webpage or copy its URL to the clipboard (for later pasting), touch and hold the link until a pop-up menu appears, and then tap Open or Copy. Tapping Open closes Numbers and opens Safari. In a crowded text box, it may take a few tries to touch the hyperlink text precisely—you may want to zoom in. (Note that none of this works for web addresses in table cells.)

Styling Objects

You can change an object's color, border, shadow, and other style attributes. An object's appearance updates as soon as you change a style option.

To style an object:

1. Tap the object to select it.
2. Tap and then tap Style.

3. To use a preset style, tap a style in the Style window **A**.
4. Tap Style Options at the bottom of the Style window.
5. To change the fill color (for text boxes and shapes), tap Fill and then tap a color **B**.

continues on next page

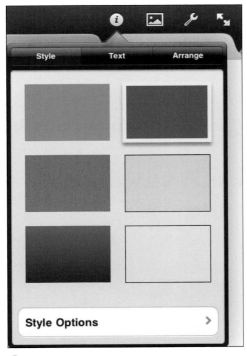

A The preset styles match the template you're using. The available style options vary by object type (text box, shape, or image). Here, the options are for a shape. To return to this window from any of the Style Options windows, tap ⬅.

B Some colors are solid, some are gradients.

6. To change the border color, width, or line type of a text box, shape, or image, tap Border and do any of the following 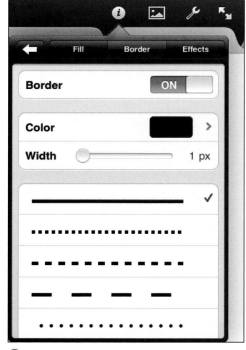 :

   ▸ To add a border or picture frame, slide Border to ON.

   ▸ To choose a border color (text boxes and shapes), tap Color and tap a color. Flick left or right to see all the colors.

   ▸ To change the thickness of the border (text boxes and shapes), drag the Width slider.

   ▸ To change the thickness of the picture frame (images), drag the Scale slider.

   ▸ To choose a line type, tap one of the lines (solid, dotted, dashed, or charcoal). Flick up or down to see all the line types.

   ▸ To choose a picture frame style (images), tap a frame style. Flick up or down to see all the frame styles.

7. To change the shadow, reflection, or opacity of a text box, shape, or image, tap Effects and do any of the following  :

   ▸ To add a shadow, slide Shadow to ON and tap a shadow style. (You should use the same shadow style for all objects, representing a single light source.)

   ▸ To make an image cast a reflection on the canvas, slide Reflection to ON and drag the slider to adjust the reflection's translucence.

   ▸ To make the object appear more or less solid, drag the Opacity slider.

C If you slide Border to OFF, the other Border options disappear and Numbers applies the default border.

D Sliding Shadow to OFF removes the shadow. Reflection works only for images. The lower the Opacity, the more transparent the object.

E Line options apply to lines and arrows only.

8. To change the color, width, arrowheads, or line type of a line or arrow, tap Line and do any of the following **E** :

   ▶ To choose a line color, tap Color and tap a color. Flick left or right to see all the colors.

   ▶ To change the thickness of the line, drag the Width slider.

   ▶ To change the arrowheads at either end of the line, tap Arrowheads and select arrowhead styles.

   ▶ To choose a line type, tap one of the lines (solid, dotted, dashed, or charcoal). Flick up or down to see all the line types.

TIP If you select multiple objects of the same type (all text boxes or all shapes, for example), you can style them at the same time. To select multiple objects, touch and hold one object and then tap the other objects.

Arranging Objects

You can move, resize, rotate, flip, layer, copy, and otherwise arrange objects on a sheet, though not all manipulations apply to all objects—you can't rotate or flip tables and charts, for example.

To select an object:

Tap the object 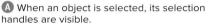.

> **TIP** If the object is a table, tap ⊙ to select the entire table.

To select multiple objects:

1. Touch and hold one object.
2. Tap the other objects **B**.

    If you tap an object accidentally, tap it again to deselect it.

> **TIP** To deselect all objects quickly, tap an empty area of the sheet.

> **TIP** To select all the objects on a sheet quickly, tap an empty area of the sheet (you may have to tap twice) and then tap Select All in the pop-up menu.

> **TIP** If the selected objects are the same type (all text boxes or all shapes, for example), you can style them at the same time (See "Styling Objects" earlier in this chapter).

Selection handle

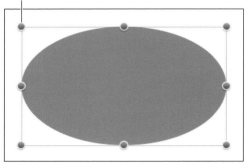

A When an object is selected, its selection handles are visible.

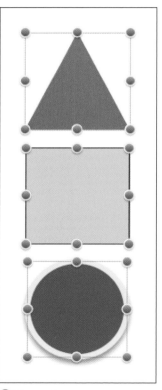

B It's usually easier to use fingertips of both hands to select multiple objects.

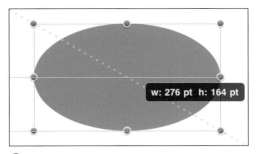

C As you resize an object, yellow edge guides appear and a pop-up label shows the dimensions of the resized object.

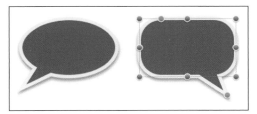

D The original shape (left) and its altered version reshaped by using only the green selection handles (right).

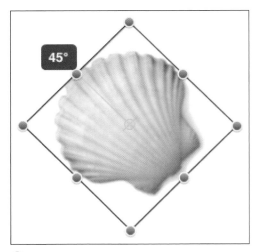

E You can rotate to any angle. During rotation, the object will "click" into position at 45-degree increments, and the edge guide will brighten. A pop-up label shows the angle of rotation.

To move an object:

Select the object and drag it.

TIP If the object is a table, drag ⬤ to move it.

TIP If you select multiple objects, you can drag them as a group.

TIP While you move or resize an object, *edge guides* flash on and off. These lines help you align the edge or center of the object with other objects on the sheet. To turn edge guides on or off, tap 🔧 > **Edge Guides**.

TIP To restrict movement to a horizontal, vertical, or diagonal (45-degree) direction, start to drag the object in the desired direction and, with a second fingertip, touch and hold an empty area on the sheet (a pop-up label indicates the drag direction).

To resize an object:

Select the object and drag its selection handles **C**.

TIP You can resize from the center of an object rather than its edges. Touch and hold a selection handle and, with a second fingertip, touch and hold an empty area on the sheet. Drag the selection handle when the Center Resize label appears.

TIP Some shapes have extra, green selection handles that reshape and resize only certain parts of the shape **D**.

To rotate an object:

Place two fingertips on an object and rotate them clockwise or counter-clockwise **E**.

After you've started the rotation, you can lift one fingertip and continue rotating by dragging a single fingertip.

TIP You can rotate text boxes, shapes, and images.

TIP If an image has transparency, you can't rotate it by holding its transparent areas.

To flip an image:

Select the image, tap ⓘ, tap Arrange, and then tap Flip Vertically or Flip Horizontally ⓕ.

To layer an object:

Select the object, tap ⓘ, tap Arrange, and then drag the Back/Front slider ⓖ.

Dragging the slider leftward moves the object toward the bottom of the stack; dragging rightward moves it toward the top.

> **TIP** If the object is a table, tap ⊙ to select the entire table.

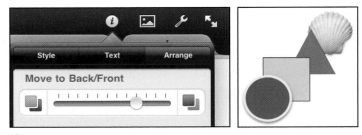

ⓕ The original image (left), flipped vertically (middle) and horizontally (right).

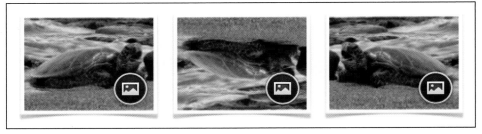

ⓖ The Back/Front slider determines how overlapping objects are stacked bottom-to-top.

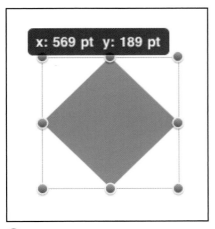

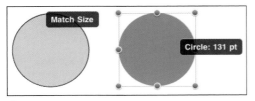

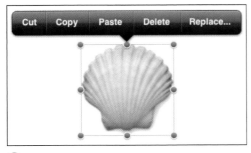

To nudge an object in one-pixel increments:

Touch and hold the object with one fingertip, and then use another fingertip to flick across the sheet in the direction that you want the object to move **H**.

TIP To nudge the object by 10, 20, or 30 pixels, flick with two, three, or four fingers.

To make two objects the same size:

1. Select the object that you want to resize, and then drag a selection handle.

2. As you drag, touch and hold another object of the desired size.

3. When the Match Size label appears, lift your fingertip from the resized object (the first object) and then the other object, or lift both fingertips at the same time **I**.

To cut, copy, or delete an object:

1. Tap the object to select it, tap it again, and then tap Cut, Copy, or Delete in the pop-up menu **J**.

2. To paste a cut or copied object, go to the destination (which can be on the same sheet, on a different sheet, or on a sheet in a different spreadsheet file), tap an empty area on the sheet, and then tap Paste in the pop-up menu.

TIP If you select multiple objects, you can cut, copy, or delete them as a group.

TIP If the object is a table, tap ⊙ to select the entire table.

H The pop-up label shows the object's x and y coordinates as you flick.

I The green circle has been resized to match the size of the yellow circle.

J Cut removes the object so that it can be moved (pasted) elsewhere. Copy copies an object so that it can be duplicated (pasted) elsewhere, leaving the original object. Delete removes the object (without placing a copy on the clipboard).

Sharing Spreadsheets

File sharing on the iPad isn't as simple as it is on Macs and PCs because the iPad has no centralized file storage area. You can't use drag-and-drop to transfer files between your iPad and computer or open documents already on your iPad in any app you choose. Instead, each iPad app keeps its data in a *sandbox*—a private storage area that other apps can't see or change. Third-party apps such as Air Sharing HD and GoodReader alleviate (but don't overcome) these restrictions, but—for now, at least—you're limited to the sharing techniques covered in this chapter (which also work for the other iWork apps, Pages and Keynote).

In This Chapter

Exporting and Importing Spreadsheets via iTunes

Using iTunes on your computer, you can:

- Export Numbers spreadsheets created on your iPad to make them available in iTunes (to, say, copy to your computer's hard drive and print or back up).

- Add spreadsheets from your computer to a special place in iTunes to import them to Numbers on your iPad over a USB connection.

Using iTunes to transfer spreadsheet files isn't like syncing photos, videos, music, and apps between your computer and your iPad. iTunes doesn't *sync* spreadsheets; it *copies* them. Every copy operation to or from your iPad is a manual, one-way process—copies exist independently of one another. For example, if you create a spreadsheet on your iPad and copy it to your computer, any changes that you make in either copy won't replace or update the other.

TIP **To export and import files, you need Mac OS X v10.5.8 or later or Windows XP SP3 or later, and iTunes 9.1 or later.**

Excel Spreadsheets

With Numbers for iPad, you can open and edit Microsoft Excel spreadsheets, but you can't create them. When you export a spreadsheet from Numbers for iPad, you can choose from only two file formats: Numbers and PDF. If you import an Excel spreadsheet and edit it in Numbers for iPad, Excel *won't* be able to read it if you export it back to your computer. A kludgy workaround: Export your Numbers for iPad spreadsheet to a Mac, open it in Numbers for Mac, and then export it in Excel format from there. You also can use third-party utilities such as pdftoexcelonline.com to convert exported PDFs to Excel files.

To export a spreadsheet from your iPad to your computer:

1. On your iPad, open Numbers.

2. In My Spreadsheets view, flick left or right to the preview of the spreadsheet that you want to export (don't open it) 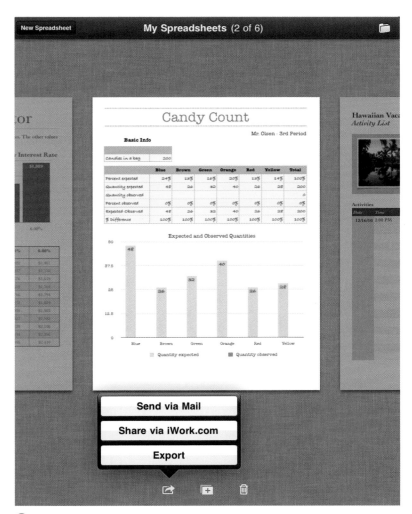.

continues on next page

A My Spreadsheets view displays all the spreadsheets that you've created or imported. Tapping the Share button opens a menu of file-sharing options.

3. Tap ![export icon], tap Export, and then tap the file format that you want to use **B**.

4. Connect your iPad to your computer via a USB cable and open iTunes on your computer.

5. In the iTunes sidebar, under Devices, click your iPad **C**.

6. In the main section of the iTunes window, click the Apps tab, and then scroll to the File Sharing section at the bottom of the window.

7. In the Apps list under File Sharing, click Numbers.

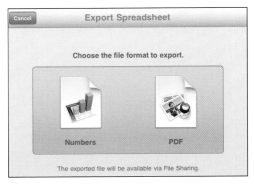

B The Numbers file format is compatible with Numbers '09 for Mac and later. PDF files can be viewed and annotated on any popular operating system.

C It may take a few moments for your iPad to appear on the iTunes sidebar.

8. In the Numbers Documents list, select the spreadsheet(s) that you want to copy to your computer **D**.

You can Control-click to select (or deselect) individual items or Shift-click to select a contiguous range of items.

9. Drag the spreadsheet(s) from the Numbers Documents list to your desktop or another folder on your computer.

or

Click Save To, navigate to the destination folder, and then click Choose (or Select Folder).

iTunes copies the spreadsheet(s) to your computer.

File Sharing

The applications listed below can transfer documents between your iPad and this computer.

Apps	Numbers Documents		
GoodReader	Book1.xls	Today 11:24 AM	16 KB
Numbers	Book2.xlsx	Today 11:25 AM	8 KB
	islands.txt	Today 10:07 AM	8 KB
	Mortgage Calculator.numbers	Today 1:35 PM	1.2 MB
	Old Faithful Eruptions.numbers	Today 1:35 PM	760 KB
	Stats Lab.pdf	Today 1:35 PM	5.5 MB
	taxes_worksheet.numbers	7/27/2010 11:49 AM	96 KB
	Travel Planner.numbers	Today 1:35 PM	704 KB
	waterfall_heights.csv	Today 10:12 AM	8 KB

Add...   Save to...

D The Numbers Documents list shows the spreadsheets that you can transfer between your computer and your iPad. To add files to this list, you can drag and drop files in it or click the Add and Save To buttons.

To import a spreadsheet from your computer to your iPad:

1. Connect your iPad to your computer via a USB cable and open iTunes on your computer.

2. In the iTunes sidebar, under Devices, click your iPad (refer to ⓒ).

3. In the main section of the iTunes window, click the Apps tab, and then scroll to the File Sharing section at the bottom of the window.

4. In the Apps list under File Sharing, click Numbers.

5. Click Add, locate and select the spreadsheet(s) that you want to import, and then click Choose (or Open).

   or

   Drag the spreadsheet(s) that you want to copy to your iPad from your desktop or from a folder window to the Numbers Documents list (refer to ⓓ).

Import Issues

Here are a few things to know about importing files from your computer to your iPad:

- Numbers for iPad can open files in these formats: Numbers '09 for Mac and later (.numbers), Microsoft Excel 97 and later (.xls, .xlsx, .xlt, .xltx, .xlsm, .xla), comma-separated values (.csv), and tab-delimited values (.txt).

- Remove any special characters (such as the forward slash, "/") from file names before you import.

- Importing a spreadsheet from Numbers for Mac or from Excel strips it permanently of features that Numbers for iPad doesn't support: 3D charts become 2D; merged cells are unmerged; missing fonts are substituted with similar ones; conditional formatting is removed; hidden rows or columns are unhidden; and steppers, sliders, pop-up menus, comments, headers, footers, and Excel scripts disappear. Apple's Numbers for iPad FAQ has a more-complete list of stripped features at support.apple.com/kb/HT4067.

Import Spreadsheet

Close Edit

	Book1
XLS	Today, 11:24 AM

	Book2
.XLS	Today, 11:25 AM

	islands
XLS	Today, 10:07 AM

	Mortgage Calculator
	Today, 1:35 PM

	Old Faithful Eruptions
	Today, 1:35 PM

	taxes_worksheet
	Jul 27, 2010 11:49 AM

E Oddly, the Import Spreadsheet window lists text (.csv and .txt) files as Excel (.xls) files.

6. On your iPad, open Numbers.

7. In My Spreadsheets view, tap 📋 in the upper-right corner of the screen (refer to **A**).

8. In the Import Spreadsheets window, tap the name of the spreadsheet you want to import **E**.

   The spreadsheet opens and Numbers reports any problems that occurred during import **F**.

> **TIP** To delete items from the Numbers Documents list, tap Edit in the Import Spreadsheets window (refer to **E**).

> **TIP** iTunes backs up your iPad automatically each time you sync. These backups include files within Numbers. If you restore from one of these backups, your Numbers for iPad files will be restored. You also may want to keep backup copies of your spreadsheets in a dedicated folder outside of iTunes.

> **TIP** To manage spreadsheets on your iPad, see "Spreadsheets" in Chapter 2.

Spreadsheet Import Warnings   Done

Numbers doesn't support some aspects of the original spreadsheet.

The font Consolas is missing. Your text might look different.

Sheet settings, such as headers and footers, were removed.

The font Arial Unicode MS is missing. Your text might look different.

F Numbers for iPad dropped some headers and made a few font substitutions when it imported this spreadsheet. If Numbers can't find a closely matching font, it uses Helvetica. For a list of fonts available on the iPad, see Apple's Numbers for iPad FAQ at support.apple.com/kb/HT4067.

Sharing Spreadsheets via iWork.com

You can post Numbers spreadsheets on Apple's iWork.com, where others (or just you) can view and download them. You must be connected to the Internet to share spreadsheets through iWork.com. You'll also need to sign in to iWork.com with an Apple ID (the same ID that you use to sign in to the iTunes store). If you don't have an Apple ID, you'll be prompted to set one up the first time you send documents to iWork.com.

When you upload a spreadsheet to iWork.com, you can optionally enter one or more email addresses and a message to alert specific people to the location of the shared file. Apple sends you and your invitees (if any) a confirmation email with the web address (URL) of the spreadsheet on iWork.com.

TIP You can't share documents on iWork.com via mountable drives or iDisk (Apple's online file-hosting service for MobileMe members).

To upload a spreadsheet to iWork.com:

1. Open Numbers on your iPad.

2. In My Spreadsheets view, flick left or right to the preview of the spreadsheet that you want to share (don't open it).

3. Tap [icon] and then tap Share via iWork. com (refer to (A) in "Exporting and Importing Spreadsheets via iTunes" earlier in this chapter).

4. Sign in, if you're not already signed in (A).

   If you don't have an Apple ID, tap "Create a new Apple ID."

(A) The first time you try to share a document using iWork.com, you must sign in and then verify your email address by clicking the Verify Now button in an email that Apple sends you.

5. In the Share via iWork.com window that opens, type the email addresses of anyone with whom you want to share the spreadsheet. If you don't want to share it, leave the To field blank. Optionally, type a message title and body in the Subject and Message fields **B**.

continues on next page

B Type or paste the email addresses of your invitees in the To field, or tap ⊕ to add people from your Contacts list. Your shared spreadsheets can be accessed only by those who click the link in the email you're sending out or by those who know its web address (URL), which you can send to them later if you wish.

6. Tap  to open the Sharing Options window, and do any of the following **C**:

   ▸ To rename the posted spreadsheet, tap its name and then type a new name. In the list of previously posted spreadsheets that appears, you can tap a name to replace it on iWork.com. When you're done, tap the Sharing Options arrow to backtrack to the other options.

   ▸ To password-protect the spreadsheet, tap Password and type the password that you want.

   ▸ To let viewers leave comments on the spreadsheet, slide Allow Comments to ON. These comments are visible to all viewers.

   ▸ Slide the Download Options sliders to choose the file format(s) in which your spreadsheet will be posted. Viewers can download the spreadsheet in any of the posted formats.

7. Tap outside the Share Options window to close it.

8. Tap Share.

9. When Numbers finishes copying the spreadsheet to iWork.com, tap View to close Numbers and open Safari and view the posted spreadsheet, or tap OK to return to Numbers **D**.

C You can apply different sharing options to each spreadsheet that you share.

D You can cancel at any time during the upload (left). After the upload completes, you have the option of viewing the uploaded spreadsheet immediately (right).

To view a shared spreadsheet on iWork.com:

1. On your Mac or PC, open the email that you received with the link to the spreadsheet **E**.

   If your email client blocks remote images by default, unblock them (typically by clicking a Show Images or Display Images link near the top of the message).

2. Click the View Document button or the *https* link, or copy and paste the URL into your browser.

continues on next page

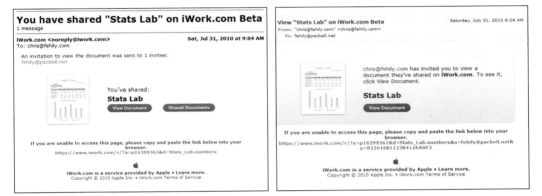

E When you share a spreadsheet on iWork.com, you'll receive an email with links that lets you view or manage your shared documents (left). Your invitees all receive a similar email (right).

3. After connecting to iWork.com, you and your visitors can view (and pan and zoom) your spreadsheet, print it, download a copy in Numbers or PDF format (according to your settings), post general notes, or add comments on yellow stickies 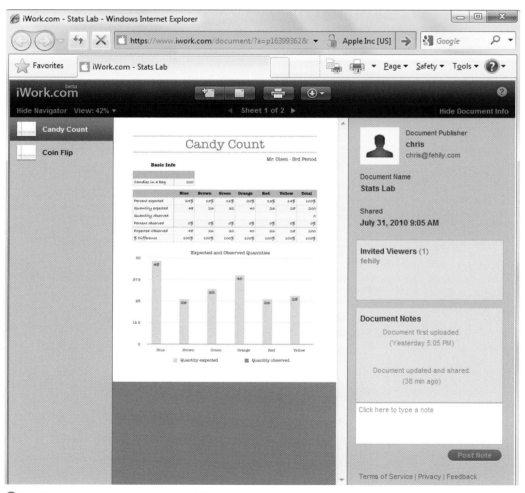.

> **TIP** iWork.com isn't suitable for collaborating with multiple authors. Visitors can't edit your spreadsheets online or upload changes.

 You'll need a modern browser to use iWork's sharing interface.

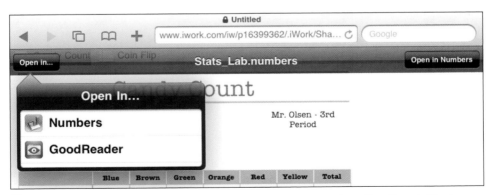

G This screen is the main switchboard for managing your shared documents. From here, you can download files, read visitors' comments, and delete documents.

To download a spreadsheet from iWork.com to your iPad:

1. In Mail on your iPad, open the email that you received with the link to the spreadsheet, and then tap Shared Documents (refer to **E**, top).

   or

   In Safari on your iPad, visit iWork.com and sign in.

2. In the list of your shared documents, tap ● next to the spreadsheet that you want to download, and then tap Numbers **G**.

   A preview of the spreadsheet opens in iWork.com.

3. In the toolbar at the top of the screen, do one of the following (if the toolbar disappears, tap anywhere on the screen to bring it back):

   ▸ Tap Open in Numbers to close Safari, launch Numbers, import the spreadsheet, and open it. When you close the spreadsheet, it will appear as the first preview in My Spreadsheets view.

   ▸ If the spreadsheet also can be opened by another app on your iPad, tap Open In and then tap any app **H**.

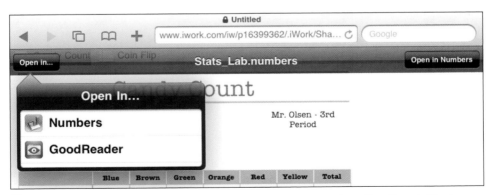

H Open In lets you open the document in any app that can read Numbers files. Open in Numbers opens the spreadsheet in its native app.

Emailing Spreadsheets

You can send spreadsheet files from your iPad as email attachments, and you can open spreadsheets emailed to you on your iPad. You must be connected to the Internet and have your email account set up on your iPad.

TIP Email setup and the Mail app are covered in the *iPad User Guide*. To read it, tap the bookmark in Safari or go to help.apple.com/ipad.

To send a spreadsheet in an email message from your iPad:

1. Open Numbers on your iPad.

2. In My Spreadsheets view, flick left or right to the preview of the spreadsheet that you want to send (don't open it).

3. Tap 📤 and then tap Send via Mail (refer to Ⓐ in "Exporting and Importing Spreadsheets via iTunes" earlier in this chapter).

4. Tap the file format you wish to send: Numbers or PDF.

5. In the email window that opens, type the email addresses of anyone to whom you want to send the spreadsheet. Optionally, type a message title and body in the Subject and body fields Ⓐ.

6. Tap Send.

Cancel	Travel Planner	Send

To: fehily@pacbell.net   ⊕

Cc/Bcc, From: chris@fehily.com

Subject: Travel Planner

Travel Planner.numbers

Ⓐ You can send a spreadsheet to yourself to put on your computer, or send it to someone else. Type or paste the email addresses of your recipients in the To field or tap ⊕ to add people from your Contacts list.

To save a spreadsheet from an email message to your iPad:

1. Open Mail on your iPad.

2. Open the message containing the attached spreadsheet file.

3. Tap the file's icon 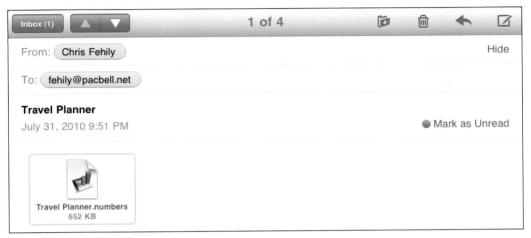.

   A preview of the spreadsheet opens in Mail.

continues on next page

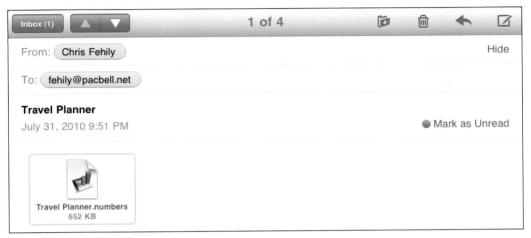

Ⓑ Attachments appear as icons in the body of the message. The file size can give you an idea of how long the download will take.

4. In the toolbar at the top of the screen, tap Open In (if the toolbar disappears, tap anywhere on the screen to bring it back) .

5. Tap Numbers to close Mail, launch Numbers, import the spreadsheet, and open it. When you close the spreadsheet, it will appear as the first preview in My Spreadsheets view.

Ⓒ The Open In menu will list Numbers and any other apps on your iPad that can open the spreadsheet.

Printing Spreadsheets

The iPad has no system-wide printing system. You can't attach it to a printer with a USB or Ethernet cable, and even if you could, the iPad has no printer drivers and Numbers for iPad has no Print command.

Most of the time, the easiest way to print your spreadsheet is to transfer it to your computer by using one of the methods covered in this chapter and then print it from there. You also can use a third-party app such as Dropbox to transfer the spreadsheet wirelessly to your computer.

Unless the target computer can open native Numbers files, you should transfer spreadsheets in PDF format. The target computer should have the same fonts installed that you used in the spreadsheet (even for PDF transfers, which don't contain embedded fonts).

A few third-party apps provide iPad-based printing by getting a document from an app and sending it to a printer—either directly to a shared network printer or wirelessly via a helper program that you install on your computer. Two popular printing apps are Air Sharing HD and PrintCentral for iPad. The easiest way to print from them is to email a PDF copy of a spreadsheet to yourself and then open it in Air Sharing or PrintCentral from the Open In menu (refer to Ⓒ).

Numbers Functions

This appendix lists all Numbers' functions, grouped by category. For details about using functions in formulas, see Chapter 4. The following Numbers for Mac functions are not available on Numbers for iPad: BIN2HEX, BIN2OCT, DEC2BIN, DEC2HEX, DEC2OCT, HEX2BIN, HEX2OCT, HYPERLINK, NUMTOBASE, OCT2BIN, and OCT2HEX.

In This Chapter

Date and Time

DATE(*year*, *month*, *day*)

Returns the date/time value for a given year, month, and day.

DATEDIF(*start-date*, *end-date*, *calc-method*)

Returns the number of days, months, or years between two dates.

DATEVALUE(*date-text*)

Converts a date text string to a date/time value. This function is provided for compatibility with other spreadsheet programs.

DAY(*date*)

Returns the day of the month for a given date/time value.

DAYNAME(*day-num*)

Returns the name of the day of the week from a date/time value or from a number. Day 1 is Sunday.

DAYS360(*start-date*, *end-date*, *use-euro-method*)

Returns the number of days between two dates based on twelve 30-day months and a 360-day year.

EDATE(*start-date*, *month-offset*)

Returns a date that is some number of months before or after a given date.

EOMONTH(*start-date*, *month-offset*)

Returns a date that is the last day of the month some number of months before or after a given date.

HOUR(*time*)

Returns the hour for a given date/time value.

MINUTE(*time*)

Returns the minutes for a given date/time value.

MONTH(*date*)

Returns the month for a given date/time value.

MONTHNAME(*month-num*)

Returns the name of the month from a number. Month 1 is January.

NETWORKDAYS(*start-date*, *end-date*, *exclude-dates*)

Returns the number of working days between two dates. Working days exclude weekends and any other specified dates.

NOW( )

Returns the current date/time value from the system clock.

SECOND(*time*)

Returns the seconds for a given date/time value.

TIME(*hours*, *minutes*, *seconds*)

Converts separate values for hours, minutes, and seconds into a date/time value.

TIMEVALUE(*time*)

Returns the time as a decimal fraction of a 24-hour day from a given date/time value or from a text string.

TODAY( )

Returns the current system date. The time is set to 12:00 a.m.

WEEKDAY(*date*, *first-day*)

Returns a number that is the day of the week for a given date.

WEEKNUM(*date*, *first-day*)

Returns the number of the week within the year for a given date.

WORKDAY(*date*, *work-days*, *exclude-dates*)

> Returns the date that is the given number of working days before or after a given date. Working days exclude weekends and any other dates specifically excluded.

YEAR(*date*)

> Returns the year for a given date/time value.

YEARFRAC(*start-date*, *end-date*, *days-basis*)

> Finds the fraction of a year represented by the number of whole days between two dates.

Duration

DUR2DAYS(*duration*)

> Converts a duration value to a number of days.

DUR2HOURS(*duration*)

> Converts a duration value to a number of hours.

DUR2MILLISECONDS(*duration*)

> Converts a duration value to a number of milliseconds.

DUR2MINUTES(*duration*)

> Converts a duration value to a number of minutes.

DUR2SECONDS(*duration*)

> Converts a duration value to a number of seconds.

DUR2WEEKS(*duration*)

> Converts a duration value to a number of weeks.

TABLE A.1 Conversion Units

Measure	Constant
Weight and Mass	
Gram	"g" (can be used with metric prefixes)
Slug	"sg"
Pound mass (avoirdupois)	"lbm"
U (atomic mass unit)	"u" (can be used with metric prefixes)
Ounce mass (avoirdupois)	"ozm"
Distance	
Meter	"m" (can be used with metric prefixes)
Statute mile	"mi"
Nautical mile	"Nmi"
Inch	"in"
Foot	"ft"
Yard	"yd"
Angstrom	"ang" (can be used with metric prefixes)
Pica (⅙ in., Postscript Pica)	"Pica"
Duration	
Year	"yr"
Week	"wk"
Day	"day"
Hour	"hr"
Minute	"mn"
Second	"sec" (can be used with metric prefixes)
Speed	
Miles per hour	"mi/h"
Miles per minute	"mi/mn"
Meters per hour	"m/h" (can be used with metric prefixes)
Meters per minute	"m/mn" (can be used with metric prefixes)

table continues on next page

TABLE A.1 *continued*

Measure	Constant
Speed *continued*	
Meters per second	"m/s" (can be used with metric prefixes)
Feet per minute	"ft/mn"
Feet per second	"ft/s"
Knot	"kt"
Pressure	
Pascal	"Pa" (can be used with metric prefixes)
Atmosphere	"atm" (can be used with metric prefixes)
Millimeters of mercury	"mmHg" (can be used with metric prefixes)
Force	
Newton	"N" (can be used with metric prefixes)
Dyne	"dyn" (can be used with metric prefixes)
Pound force	"lbf"
Energy	
Joule	"J" (can be used with metric prefixes)
Erg	"e" (can be used with metric prefixes)
Thermodynamic calorie	"c" (can be used with metric prefixes)
IT calorie	"cal" (can be used with metric prefixes)
Electron volt	"eV" (can be used with metric prefixes)
Horsepower-hour	"HPh"
Watt-hour	"Wh" (can be used with metric prefixes)
Foot-pound	"flb"
BTU	"BTU"

table continues on next page

DURATION(*weeks*, *days*, *hours*, *minutes*, *seconds*, *milliseconds*)

Combines separate values for weeks, days, hours, minutes, seconds, and milliseconds and returns a duration value.

STRIPDURATION(*any-value*)

Evaluates a given value and returns either the number of days represented, if a duration value, or the given value. This function is included for compatibility with other spreadsheet applications.

Engineering

BASETONUM(*convert-string*, *base*)

Converts a number of the specified base into a number in base 10.

BESSELJ(*any-x-value*, *n-value*)

Returns the integer Bessel function $J_n(x)$.

BESSELY(*pos-x-value*, *n-value*)

Returns the integer Bessel function $Y_n(x)$.

BIN2DEC(*binary-string*, *convert-length*)

Converts a binary number to the corresponding decimal number.

CONVERT(*convert-num*, *from-unit*, *to-unit*)

Converts a number from one measurement system to its corresponding value in another measurement system. **Table A.1** (opposite page) lists the valid values for *from-unit* and *to-unit* (all constants are case-sensitive). The metric constants in Table A.1 can be prefixed with the multiplier constants listed in **Table A.2** (page 125); for example, prefixing "m" (meters) with "k" (kilo) yields "km" (kilometers).

DELTA(*compare-from*, *compare-to*)

Determines whether two values are exactly equal.

ERF(*lower*, *upper*)

Returns the error function integrated between two values.

ERFC(*lower*)

Returns the complementary ERF function integrated between a given lower bound and infinity.

GESTEP(*compare-num*, *step-number*)

Determines whether one value is greater than or exactly equal to another value.

HEX2DEC(*hex-string*, *convert-length*)

Converts a hexadecimal number to the corresponding decimal number.

OCT2DEC(*octal-string*, *convert-length*)

Converts an octal number to the corresponding decimal number.

Financial

ACCRINT(*issue*, *first*, *settle*, *annual-rate*, *par*, *frequency*, *days-basis*)

Calculates the accrued interest added to the purchase price of a security and paid to the seller when the security pays periodic interest.

ACCRINTM(*issue*, *settle*, *annual-rate*, *par*, *days-basis*)

Calculates the total accrued interest added to the purchase price of a security and paid to the seller when the security pays interest only at maturity.

BONDDURATION(*settle*, *maturity*, *annual-rate*, *annual-yield*, *frequency*, *days-basis*)

Calculates the weighted average of the present value of the cash flows for an assumed par value of $100.

TABLE A.1 *continued*

Measure	Constant
Power	
Horsepower	"HP"
Watt	"W" (can be used with metric prefixes)
Magnetism	
Tesla	"T" (can be used with metric prefixes)
Gauss	"ga" (can be used with metric prefixes)
Temperature	
Degrees Celsius	"C"
Degrees Fahrenheit	"F"
Kelvins	"K" (can be used with metric prefixes)
Liquid	
Teaspoon	"tsp"
Tablespoon	"tbs"
Fluid ounce	"oz"
Cup	"cup"
U.S. pint	"pt"
U.K. pint	"uk_pt"
Quart	"qt"
Gallon	"gal"
Liter	"l" (can be used with metric prefixes)

TABLE A.2 Metric Prefixes

Measure (Multiplier)	Constant
exa (1E+18)	"E"
peta (1E+15)	"P"
tera (1E+12)	"T"
giga (1E+09)	"G"
mega (1E+06)	"M"
kilo (1E+03)	"k"
hecto (1E+02)	"h"
deca (1E+01)	"e"
deci (1E-01)	"d"
centi (1E-02)	"c"
milli (1E-03)	"m"
micro (1E-06)	"u" or "μ"
nano (1E-09)	"n"
pico (1E-12)	"p"
femto (1E-15)	"f"
atto (1E-18)	"a"

BONDMDURATION(*settle, maturity, annual-rate, annual-yield, frequency, days-basis*)

Calculates the modified weighted average of the present value of the cash flows for an assumed par value of $100.

COUPDAYBS(*settle, maturity, frequency, days-basis*)

Returns the number of days between the beginning of the coupon period in which settlement occurs and the settlement date.

COUPDAYS(*settle, maturity, frequency, days-basis*)

Returns the number of days in the coupon period in which settlement occurs.

COUPDAYSNC(*settle, maturity, frequency, days-basis*)

Returns the number of days between the settlement date and the end of the coupon period in which settlement occurs.

COUPNUM(*settle, maturity, frequency, days-basis*)

Returns the number of coupons remaining to be paid between the settlement date and the maturity date.

CUMIPMT(*periodic-rate, num-periods, present-value, starting-per, ending-per, when-due*)

Returns the total interest included in loan or annuity payments over a chosen time interval based on fixed periodic payments and a fixed interest rate.

CUMPRINC(*periodic-rate, num-periods, present-value, starting-per, ending-per, cum-when-due*)

Returns the total principal included in loan or annuity payments over a chosen time interval based on fixed periodic payments and a fixed interest rate.

DB(*cost*, *salvage*, *life*, *depr-period*, *first-year-months*)

> Returns the amount of depreciation of an asset for a specified period using the fixed-declining balance method.

DDB(*cost*, *salvage*, *life*, *depr-period*, *depr-factor*)

> Returns the amount of depreciation of an asset based on a specified depreciation rate.

DISC(*settle*, *maturity*, *price*, *redemption*, *days-basis*)

> Returns the annual discount rate of a security that pays no interest and is sold at a discount to its redemption value.

EFFECT(*nominal-rate*, *num-periods-year*)

> Returns the effective annual interest rate from the nominal annual interest rate based on the number of compounding periods per year.

FV(*periodic-rate*, *num-periods*, *payment*, *present-value*, *when-due*)

> Returns the future value of an investment based on a series of regular periodic cash flows (payments of a constant amount and all cash flows at constant intervals) and a fixed interest rate.

INTRATE(*settle*, *maturity*, *invest-amount*, *redemption*, *days-basis*)

> Returns the effective annual interest rate for a security that pays interest only at maturity.

IPMT(*periodic-rate*, *period*, *num-periods*, *present-value*, *future-value*, *when-due*)

> Returns the interest portion of a specified loan or annuity payment based on fixed, periodic payments and a fixed interest rate.

IRR(*flows-range*, *estimate*)

>Returns the internal rate of return for an investment that is based on a series of potentially irregular cash flows that occur at regular time intervals.

ISPMT(*annual-rate*, *period*, *num-periods*, *present-value*)

>Returns the interest portion of a specified loan or annuity payment based on fixed, periodic payments and a fixed interest rate. This function is provided for compatibility with tables imported from other spreadsheet applications.

MIRR(*flows-range*, *finance-rate*, *reinvest-rate*)

>Returns the modified internal rate of return for an investment that is based on a series of potentially irregular cash flows that occur at regular time intervals. The rate earned on positive cash flows and the rate paid to finance negative cash flows can differ.

NOMINAL(*effective-int-rate*, *num-periods-year*)

>Returns the nominal annual interest rate from the effective annual interest rate based on the number of compounding periods per year.

NPER(*periodic-rate*, *payment*, *present-value*, *future-value*, *when-due*)

>Returns the number of payment periods for a loan or annuity based on a series of regular periodic cash flows (payments of a constant amount and all cash flows at constant intervals) and a fixed interest rate.

NPV(*periodic-discount-rate*, *cash-flow*, *cash-flow...*)

>Returns the net present value of an investment based on a series of potentially irregular cash flows that occur at regular time intervals.

PMT(*periodic-rate*, *num-periods*, *present-value*, *future-value*, *when-due*)

> Returns the fixed periodic payment for a loan or annuity based on a series of regular periodic cash flows (payments of a constant amount and all cash flows at constant intervals) and a fixed interest rate.

PPMT(*periodic-rate*, *period*, *num-periods*, *present-value*, *future-value*, *when-due*)

> Returns the principal portion of a specified loan or annuity payment based on fixed periodic payments and a fixed interest rate.

PRICE(*settle*, *maturity*, *annual-rate*, *annual-yield*, *redemption*, *frequency*, *days-basis*)

> Returns the price of a security that pays periodic interest per $100 of redemption (par) value.

PRICEDISC(*settle*, *maturity*, *annual-yield*, *redemption*, *days-basis*)

> Returns the price of a security that is sold at a discount to redemption value and does not pay interest per $100 of redemption (par) value.

PRICEMAT(*settle*, *maturity*, *issue*, *annual-rate*, *annual-yield*, *days-basis*)

> Returns the price of a security that pays interest only at maturity per $100 of redemption (par) value.

PV(*periodic-rate*, *num-periods*, *payment*, *future-value*, *when-due*)

> Returns the present value of an investment or annuity based on a series of regular periodic cash flows (payments of a constant amount and all cash flows at constant intervals) and a fixed interest rate.

RATE(*num-periods*, *payment*, *present-value*, *future-value*, *when-due*, *estimate*)

> Returns the interest rate of an investment, loan, or annuity based on a series of regular periodic cash flows (payments of a constant amount and all cash flows at constant intervals) and a fixed interest rate.

RECEIVED(*settle*, *maturity*, *invest-amount*, *annual-rate*, *days-basis*)

> Returns the maturity value for a security that pays interest only at maturity.

SLN(*cost*, *salvage*, *life*)

> Returns the amount of depreciation of an asset for a single period using the straight-line method.

SYD(*cost*, *salvage*, *life*, *depr-period*)

> Returns the amount of depreciation of an asset for a specified period using the sum-of-the-years-digits method.

VDB(*cost*, *salvage*, *life*, *starting-per*, *ending-per*, *depr-factor*, *no-switch*)

> Returns the amount of depreciation of an asset over a chosen time interval, based on a specified depreciation rate.

YIELD(*settle*, *maturity*, *annual-rate*, *price*, *redemption*, *frequency*, *days-basis*)

> Returns the effective annual interest rate for a security that pays regular periodic interest.

YIELDDISC(*settle*, *maturity*, *price*, *redemption*, *days-basis*)

> Returns the effective annual interest rate for a security that is sold at a discount to redemption value and pays no interest.

YIELDMAT(*settle*, *maturity*, *issue*, *annual-rate*, *price*, *days-basis*)

> Returns the effective annual interest rate for a security that pays interest only at maturity.

Logical and Information

AND(*test-expression*, *test-expression*...)

> Returns TRUE if all arguments are true; otherwise, returns FALSE.

FALSE( )

> Returns the Boolean value FALSE. This function is included for compatibility with tables imported from other spreadsheet applications.

IF(*if-expression*, *if-true*, *if-false*)

> Returns one of two values depending on whether a specified expression evaluates to a Boolean value of TRUE or FALSE.

IFERROR(*any-expression*, *if-error*)

> Returns a value that you specify if a given value evaluates to an error; otherwise, returns the given value.

ISBLANK(*cell*)

> Returns TRUE if the specified cell is empty; otherwise, returns FALSE.

ISERROR(*any-expression*)

> Returns TRUE if a given expression evaluates to an error; otherwise, returns FALSE.

ISEVEN(*num*)

> Returns TRUE if the value is even (leaves no remainder when divided by 2); otherwise, returns FALSE.

ISODD(*num*)

Returns TRUE if the value is odd (leaves a remainder when divided by 2); otherwise, returns FALSE.

NOT(*any-expression*)

Returns the opposite of the Boolean value of a specified expression.

OR(*any-expression*, *any-expression*...)

Returns TRUE if any argument is true; otherwise, returns FALSE.

TRUE( )

Returns the Boolean value TRUE. This function is included for compatibility with tables imported from other spreadsheet applications.

Numeric

ABS(*num-dur*)

Returns the absolute value of a number or duration.

CEILING(*num-to-round*, *multiple-factor*)

Rounds a number away from zero to the nearest multiple of the specified factor.

COMBIN(*total-items*, *group-size*)

Returns the number of different ways you can combine a number of items into groups of a specific size, ignoring the order within the groups.

EVEN(*num-to-round*)

Rounds a number away from zero to the next even number.

EXP(*exponent*)

Returns *e* (the base of natural logarithms) raised to the specified power.

FACT(*fact-num*)

Returns the factorial of a number.

FACTDOUBLE(*fact-num*)

Returns the double factorial of a number.

FLOOR(*num-to-round*, *factor*)

Rounds a number toward zero to the nearest multiple of the specified factor.

GCD(*num-value*, *num-value...*)

Returns the greatest common divisor of the specified numbers.

INT(*num-to-round*)

Returns the nearest integer that is less than or equal to the number.

LCM(*num-value*, *num-value...*)

Returns the least common multiple of the specified numbers.

LN(*pos-num*)

Returns the natural logarithm of a number, the power to which e must be raised to result in the number.

LOG(*pos-num*, *base*)

Returns the logarithm of a number using a specified base.

LOG10(*pos-num*)

Returns the base-10 logarithm of a number.

MOD(*dividend*, *divisor*)

Returns the remainder from a division.

MROUND(*num-to-round*, *factor*)

Rounds a number to the nearest multiple of a specified factor.

MULTINOMIAL(*non-neg-num*, *non-neg-num...*)

Returns the closed form of the multinomial coefficient of the given numbers.

ODD(*num-to-round*)

Rounds a number away from zero to the next odd number.

PI( )

Returns the approximate value of π (pi), the ratio of a circle's circumference to its diameter.

POWER(*number*, *exponent*)

Returns a number raised to a power.

PRODUCT(*num-value*, *num-value...*)

Returns the product of one or more numbers.

QUOTIENT(*dividend*, *divisor*)

Returns the integer quotient of two numbers.

RAND( )

Returns a uniform random number that is greater than or equal to 0 and less than 1.

RANDBETWEEN(*lower*, *upper*)

Returns a random integer within the specified range, inclusive.

ROMAN(*arabic-num*, *roman-style*)

Converts a number to Roman numerals.

ROUND(*num-to-round*, *digits*)

Returns a number rounded to the specified number of places.

ROUNDDOWN(*num-to-round*, *digits*)

Returns a number rounded toward zero (rounded down) to the specified number of places.

ROUNDUP(*num-to-round*, *digits*)

Returns a number rounded away from zero (rounded up) to the specified number of places.

SIGN(*num*)

Returns 1 when a given number is positive, –1 when it is negative, or 0 when it is zero.

SQRT(*num*)

   Returns the square root of a number.

SQRTPI(*non-neg-number*)

   Returns the square root of a number multiplied by π (pi).

SUM(*num-date-dur*, *num-date-dur*...)

   Returns the sum of a collection of numbers.

SUMIF(*test-values*, *condition*, *sum-values*)

   Returns the sum of a collection of numbers, including only numbers that satisfy a specified condition.

SUMIFS(*sum-values*, *test-values*, *condition*, *test-values*..., *condition*...)

   Returns the sum of the cells in a collection where the test values meet the given conditions.

SUMPRODUCT(*range*, *range*...)

   Returns the sum of the products of corresponding numbers in one or more ranges.

SUMSQ(*num-value*, *num-value*...)

   Returns the sum of the squares of a collection of numbers.

SUMX2MY2(*set-1-values*, *set-2-values*)

   Returns the sum of the difference of the squares of corresponding values in two collections.

SUMX2PY2(*set-1-values*, *set-2-values*)

   Returns the sum of the squares of corresponding values in two collections.

SUMXMY2(*set-1-values*, *set-2-values*)

   Returns the sum of the squares of the differences between corresponding values in two collections.

TRUNC(*number*, *digits*)

   Truncates a number to the specified number of digits.

Reference

ADDRESS(*row, column, addr-type, addr-style, table*)

> Constructs a cell address string from separate row, column, and table identifiers.

AREAS(*areas*)

> Returns the number of ranges the function references.

CHOOSE(*index, value, value...*)

> Returns a value from a collection of values based on a specified index value.

COLUMN(*cell*)

> Returns the column number of the column containing a specified cell.

COLUMNS(*range*)

> Returns the number of columns included in a specified range of cells.

HLOOKUP(*search-for, rows-range, return-row, close-match*)

> Returns a value from a range of rows by using the top row of values to pick a column and a row number to pick a row within that column.

INDEX(*range, row-index, column-index, area-index*)

> Returns the value in the cell located at the intersection of the specified row and column within a range of cells.

INDIRECT(*addr-string, addr-style*)

> Returns the contents of a cell or range referenced by an address specified as a string.

LOOKUP(*search-for*, *search-where*, *result-values*)

> Finds a match for a given search value in one range and then returns the value in the cell with the same relative position in a second range.

MATCH(*search-for*, *search-where*, *matching-method*)

> Returns the position of a value within a range.

OFFSET(*base*, *row-offset*, *column-offset*, *rows*, *columns*)

> Returns a range of cells that is the specified number of rows and columns away from the specified base cell.

ROW(*cell*)

> Returns the row number of the row containing a specified cell.

ROWS(*range*)

> Returns the number of rows included in a specified range of cells.

TRANSPOSE(*range-array*)

> Returns a vertical range of cells as a horizontal range of cells, or vice versa.

VLOOKUP(*search-for*, *columns-range*, *return-column*, *close-match*)

> Returns a value from a range of columns by using the left column of values to pick a row and a column number to pick a column in that row.

Statistical

AVEDEV(*num-date-dur*, *num-date-dur*...)

> Returns the average of the difference of a collection of numbers from their average (arithmetic mean).

AVERAGE(*num-date-dur*, *num-date-dur*...)

Returns the average (arithmetic mean) of a collection of numbers.

AVERAGEA(*value*, *value*...)

Returns the average (arithmetic mean) of a collection of values, including text and Boolean values.

AVERAGEIF(*test-values*, *condition*, *avg-values*)

Returns the average (arithmetic mean) of the cells in a range that meet a given condition.

AVERAGEIFS(*avg-values*, *test-values*, *condition*, *test-values*..., *condition*...)

Returns the average (arithmetic mean) of the cells in a collection that meet all the given conditions.

BETADIST(*x-value*, *alpha*, *beta*, *x-lower*, *x-upper*)

Returns the cumulative beta distribution probability value.

BETAINV(*probability*, *alpha*, *beta*, *x-lower*, *x-upper*)

Returns the inverse of the given cumulative beta distribution probability value.

BINOMDIST(*success-num*, *trials*, *prob-success*, *form-type*)

Returns the individual term binomial distribution probability of the specified form.

CHIDIST(*non-neg-x-value*, *degrees-freedom*)

Returns the one-tailed probability of the chi-square distribution.

CHIINV(*probability*, *degrees-freedom*)

Returns the inverse of the one-tailed probability of the chi-square distribution.

CHITEST(*actual-values*, *expected-values*)

Returns the value from the chi-square distribution for the given data.

CONFIDENCE(*alpha*, *stdev*, *sample-size*)

Returns a value for creating a statistical confidence interval for a sample from a population with a known standard deviation.

CORREL(*y-values*, *x-values*)

Returns the correlation between two collections using linear regression analysis.

COUNT(*value*, *value*...)

Returns the number of its arguments that contain numbers, numeric expressions, or dates.

COUNTA(*value*, *value*...)

Returns the number of its arguments that are not empty.

COUNTBLANK(*range*)

Returns the number of cells in a range that are empty.

COUNTIF(*test-array*, *condition*)

Returns the number of cells in a range that satisfy a given condition.

COUNTIFS(*test-values*, *condition*, *test-values*..., *condition*...)

Returns the number of cells in one or more ranges that satisfy given conditions (one condition per range).

COVAR(*sample-1-values*, *sample-2-values*)

Returns the covariance of two collections.

CRITBINOM(*trials*, *prob-success*, *alpha*)

Returns the smallest value for which the cumulative binomial distribution is greater than or equal to a given value.

DEVSQ(*num-value, num-value…*)

Returns the sum of the squares of deviations of a collection of numbers from their average (arithmetic mean).

EXPONDIST(*non-neg-x-value, lambda, form-type*)

Returns the exponential distribution of the specified form.

FDIST(*non-neg-x-value, d-f-numerator, d-f-denominator*)

Returns the F probability distribution.

FINV(*prob, d-f-numerator, d-f-denominator*)

Returns the inverse of the F probability distribution.

FORECAST(*x-num-date-dur, y-values, x-values*)

Returns the forecasted y value for a given x value based on sample values using linear regression analysis.

FREQUENCY(*data-values, interval-values*)

Returns an array of how often data values occur within a range of interval values.

GAMMADIST(*non-neg-x-value, alpha, beta, form-type*)

Returns the gamma distribution in the specified form.

GAMMAINV(*probability, alpha, beta*)

Returns the inverse gamma cumulative distribution.

GAMMALN(*pos-x-value*)

Returns the natural logarithm of the gamma function, $\Gamma(x)$.

GEOMEAN(*pos-num, pos-num…*)

Returns the geometric mean.

HARMEAN(*pos-num, pos-num…*)

Returns the harmonic mean.

INTERCEPT(*y-values*, *x-numbers*)

Returns the y-intercept of the best-fit line for the collection using linear regression analysis.

LARGE(*num-date-dur-set*, *ranking*)

Returns the nth-largest value within a collection. The largest value is ranked number 1.

LINEST(*known-y-values*, *known-x-values*, *nonzero-y-intercept*, *more-stats*)

Returns an array of the statistics for a straight line that best fits the given data using the least-squares method.

LOGINV(*probability*, *mean*, *stdev*)

Returns the inverse of the log-normal cumulative distribution function of x.

LOGNORMDIST(*pos-x-value*, *mean*, *stdev*)

Returns the log-normal distribution.

MAX(*value*, *value*...)

Returns the largest number in a collection.

MAXA(*value*, *value*...)

Returns the largest number in a collection of values that can include text and Boolean values.

MEDIAN(*num-date-dur*, *num-date-dur*...)

Returns the median value in a collection of numbers. The median is the value where half the numbers in the collection are less than the median and half are greater.

MIN(*value*, *value*...)

Returns the smallest number in a collection.

MINA(*value*, *value*...)

Returns the smallest number in a collection of values that can include text and Boolean values.

MODE(*num-date-dur, num-date-dur...*)

Returns the most frequently occurring value in a collection of numbers.

NEGBINOMDIST(*f-num, s-num, prob-success*)

Returns the negative binomial distribution.

NORMDIST(*num, average, stdev, form-type*)

Returns the normal distribution of the specified function form.

NORMINV(*probability, average, stdev*)

Returns the inverse of the cumulative normal distribution.

NORMSDIST(*num*)

Returns the standard normal distribution.

NORMSINV(*probability*)

Returns the inverse of the cumulative standard normal distribution.

PERCENTILE(*num-date-dur-set, percentile-value*)

Returns the value within a collection that corresponds to a particular percentile.

PERCENTRANK(*num-date-dur-set, num-date-dur, significance*)

Returns the rank of a value in a collection as a percentage of the collection.

PERMUT(*num-objects, num-elements*)

Returns the number of permutations for a given number of objects that can be selected from a total number of objects.

POISSON(*events, average, form-type*)

Returns the probability that a specific number of events will occur using the Poisson distribution.

PROB(*num-set*, *probability-values*, *lower*, *upper*)

Returns the probability of a range of values if you know the probabilities of the individual values.

QUARTILE(*num-set*, *quartile-num*)

Returns the value for the specified quartile of a given collection.

RANK(*num-date-dur*, *num-date-dur-set*, *largest-is-high*)

Returns the rank of a number within a range of numbers.

SLOPE(*y-values*, *x-values*)

Returns the slope of the best-fit line for the collection using linear regression analysis.

SMALL(*num-date-dur-set*, *ranking*)

Returns the nth-smallest value within a range. The smallest value is ranked number 1.

STANDARDIZE(*num*, *average*, *stdev*)

Returns a normalized value from a distribution characterized by a given mean and standard deviation.

STDEV(*num-date-dur*, *num-date-dur...*)

Returns the standard deviation, a measure of dispersion, of a collection of values based on their sample (unbiased) variance.

STDEVA(*value*, *value...*)

Returns the standard deviation, a measure of dispersion, of a collection of values that can include text and Boolean values, based on the sample (unbiased) variance.

STDEVP(*num-date-dur*, *num-date-dur...*)

Returns the standard deviation, a measure of dispersion, of a collection of values based on their population (true) variance.

STDEVPA(*value, value…*)

Returns the standard deviation, a measure of dispersion, of a collection of values that can include text and Boolean values, based on the population (true) variance.

TDIST(*non-neg-x-value, degrees-freedom, tails*)

Returns the probability from the Student's t-distribution.

TINV(*probability, degrees-freedom*)

Returns the t value (a function of the probability and degrees of freedom) from the Student's t-distribution.

TTEST(*sample-1-values, sample-2-values, tails, test-type*)

Returns the probability associated with a Student's t-test, based on the t-distribution function.

VAR(*num-date, num-date…*)

Returns the sample (unbiased) variance, a measure of dispersion, of a collection of values.

VARA(*value, value…*)

Returns the sample (unbiased) variance, a measure of dispersion, of a collection of values that can include text and Boolean values.

VARP(*num-date, num-date…*)

Returns the population (true) variance, a measure of dispersion, of a collection of values.

VARPA(*value, value…*)

Returns the sample (unbiased) variance, a measure of dispersion, of a collection of values that can include text and Boolean values.

ZTEST(*num-date-dur-set*, *num-date-dur*, *stdev*)

> Returns the one-tailed probability value of the Z-test.

Text

CHAR(*code-number*)

> Returns the character that corresponds to a decimal Unicode character code.

CLEAN(*text*)

> Removes most common nonprinting characters (Unicode character codes 0–31) from text.

CODE(*code-string*)

> Returns the decimal Unicode number of the first character in a specified string.

CONCATENATE(*string*, *string*...)

> Joins (concatenates) strings.

DOLLAR(*num*, *places*)

> Returns a string formatted as a dollar amount from a given number.

EXACT(*string-1*, *string-2*)

> Returns TRUE if the argument strings are identical in case and content.

FIND(*search-string*, *source-string*, *start-pos*)

> Returns the starting position of one string within another.

FIXED(*num*, *places*, *no-commas*)

> Rounds a number to the specified number of decimal places and then returns the result as a string value.

LEFT(*source-string*, *string-length*)

> Returns a string consisting of the specified number of characters from the left end of a given string.

LEN(*source-string*)

Returns the number of characters in a string.

LOWER(*source-string*)

Returns a string that is entirely lowercase, regardless of the case of the characters in the specified string.

MID(*source-string*, *start-pos*, *string-length*)

Returns a string consisting of the given number of characters from a string starting at the specified position.

PROPER(*source-string*)

Returns a string where the first letter of each word is uppercase and all remaining characters are lowercase, regardless of the case of the characters in the specified string.

REPLACE(*source-string*, *start-pos*, *replace-length*, *new-string*)

Returns a string where a specified number of characters of a given string have been replaced with a new string.

REPT(*source-string*, *repeat-number*)

Returns a string that contains a given string repeated a specified number of times.

RIGHT(*source-string*, *string-length*)

Returns a string consisting of the given number of characters from the right end of a specified string.

SEARCH(*search-string*, *source-string*, *start-pos*)

Returns the starting position of one string within another, ignoring case and allowing wildcards.

SUBSTITUTE(*source-string*, *existing-string*, *new-string*, *occurrence*)

Returns a string where the specified characters of a given string have been replaced with a new string.

T(*cell*)

Returns the text contained in a cell. This function is included for compatibility with tables imported from other spreadsheet applications.

TRIM(*source-string*)

Returns a string based on a given string, after removing extra spaces.

UPPER(*source-string*)

Returns a string that is entirely uppercase, regardless of the case of the characters in the specified string.

VALUE(*source-string*)

Returns a number value even if the argument is formatted as text.

Trigonometric

ACOS(*num*)

Returns the inverse cosine (arccosine) of a number.

ACOSH(*num*)

Returns the inverse hyperbolic cosine (hyperbolic arccosine) of a number.

ASIN(*num*)

Returns the arcsine (the inverse sine) of a number.

ASINH(*num*)

Returns the inverse hyperbolic sine of a number.

ATAN(*num*)

Returns the inverse tangent (arctangent) of a number.

ATAN2(*x-point*, *y-point*)

Returns the angle, relative to the positive x-axis, of the line passing through the origin and the specified point.

ATANH(*num*)

Returns the inverse hyperbolic tangent of a number.

COS(*radian-angle*)

Returns the cosine of an angle that is expressed in radians.

COSH(*num*)

Returns the hyperbolic cosine of a number.

DEGREES(*radian-angle*)

Returns the number of degrees in an angle expressed in radians.

RADIANS(*degree-angle*)

Returns the number of radians in an angle expressed in degrees.

SIN(*radian-angle*)

Returns the sine of an angle that is expressed in radians.

SINH(*num*)

Returns the hyperbolic sine of the specified number.

TAN(*radian-angle*)

Returns the tangent of an angle that is expressed in radians.

TANH(*num*)

Returns the hyperbolic tangent of the specified number.

Index

WATCH READ CREATE

Meet Creative Edge.

A new resource of unlimited books, videos and tutorials for creatives from the world's leading experts.

Creative Edge is your one stop for inspiration, answers to technical questions and ways to stay at the top of your game so you can focus on what you do best—being creative.

All for only $24.99 per month for access—any day any time you need it.

creative edge

peachpit.com/creativeedge